Corruption in Nigeria

The Fight and Movement to Cure the Malady

Mazi A. Kanu Oji
and
Valerie U. Oji

University Press of America,® Inc.
Lanham · Boulder · New York · Toronto · Plymouth, UK

Copyright © 2010 by
University Press of America,® Inc.
4501 Forbes Boulevard
Suite 200
Lanham, Maryland 20706
UPA Acquisitions Department (301) 459-3366

Estover Road
Plymouth PL6 7PY
United Kingdom

Library of Congress Control Number: 2010933274
ISBN: 978-0-7618-5217-9 (paperback : alk. paper)
eISBN: 978-0-7618-5218-6

™The paper used in this publication meets the minimum
requirements of American National Standard for Information
Sciences—Permanence of Paper for Printed Library Materials,
ANSI Z39.48-1992

DEDICATION

Dedicated to the beautiful continent of Africa in all her past glory, current struggles and future promise. Sometimes misunderstood, oft times underrated, yet unwavering faith ascertains that God's plan for Africa will be realized.

Dr. Valerie U. Oji

CONTENTS

LIST OF FIGURES - APPENDIX

LIST OF TABLES

FOREWORD

There are many well-meaning critics of the problem of corruption in Nigeria, but few have taken the time to study it. Mazi Oji and Valerie Oji, in *Corruption in Nigeria: The Fight and Movement to Cure the Malady,* provide a candid analysis of the problem of corruption that spans from before Nigeria's independence as a nation-state in 1960 through nearly five decades of successive cycles of civilian and military control of the Federal Republic. The authors dispel any misapprehension about the devastating affect corruption has had on national development in Nigeria; they shed light on its devastating impact on both infra-structural and cultural developments.

Nigeria has great potential for becoming one of the world's leading nation-states, but its leaders must control and harness its human capital and natural resources for the benefit of the nation-state itself. This historically has involved a struggle on two fronts. The first was waged against colonial mandates from outside the country where achieving national independence was clearly the political objective. The second struggle has been a struggle from within the moral and ethical culture of the nation itself. This second front is the concern of the authors in this book. They provide graphic examples of corruption in high places by political leaders holding offices in the national government; they argue that corruption has escaped a cure since its beginning as a nation-state; and they express their discontent with its visible dysfunctional consequences inside the country. They also call our attention to what this ongoing issue has meant in the creation of a negative image of Nigeria in the global community.

The authors, with respect to the second leg of their tripod approach, point to the role of the Ministry of Education in the creation of programs to promote civic values of integrity, honesty, patriotism, and the like. The Re-branding Nigeria Project is an example of the national effort. The third prong of the authors' approach reaches deep into the Nigerian society itself and has broad implications for development and change. For, as they disclose, billions of naira have been misdirected from the Nigeria's national treasury by political leaders who placed their personal interest over the interest of the nation. There is the question of what happens to a Minister of a government agency who is convicted of embezzling millions of naira. Though convicted, will he be forced to pay back the money; if he appeals, will he find a way to leave the country without any restitution made; and will he be allowed to return several years later with impunity. These are critical questions which the authors grapple with.

They call our attention to a notable bright light in the struggle against corruption, crime, and fraud in the medical field in Nigeria, the accomplishments of Dora Akunyili. Her successful leadership, over a period of seven years, in instituting and enforcing laws governing health policies, together with the war she fought against the sale of counterfeit drugs and illegal sale of substandard medicine, were no less than a social revolution in the health industry. Her success against the powerful resistors in both the informal and formal markets and among private individuals must be considered as a microcosm of what is possible in other sectors of the Nigerian society, as well as one that can be emulated in other countries, which is why the authors devote considerable time on Akunyili's promotion of ethical standards and self sacrifice as a paradigm of change outside the traditional political leadership. Targeting the general Nigerian culture itself, they propose a transformational model to introduce change, one in which change is expected to move from the top down. That is, they hold that change must occur first in the leadership and be manifested in the political leaders' exhibition of ethical behavior and their political will to fight against the abusive use of power and unethical corrupt behavior of subordinates: These attributes, they proffer in the final chapter, are most visible in the servant leader., They cite, as examples, General Colin Powell, the former Secretary of State of the United States, and the current President of Nigeria, Umaru Yar'Adua. The President, by revealing to the public consistently for ten years his assets, may inspire similar behavior by other leaders. It is a laudable beginning.

The ordinary Nigerian citizen expects much from its leadership and from those in powerful positions. This includes the expectation to pay reasonable cost for medical treatment and medicine or to have access to the best available health care (under certain circumstances to believe that they have a right). To the misfortune of many Nigerian citizens, the authors cite problems connected with the misappropriation of funds intended for basic health care delivery in diseases (malaria, polio) or for the treatment of other globally connected diseases (HIV/AIDS). The problem extends to the deleterious affect of fraud in the circulation of illegal and fake drugs. These problems must be rectified. They leave no doubt why the country cannot afford to have a Minister of Health that embezzles from funds intended to benefit the common man.

This work is a balanced perspective on the baneful effects of corruption in Nigeria. The country, the most populous in Africa, with an increasingly growing population that is placing greater demand on the government to provide goods and services, must find ways to cope with the problem. Superficial strategies to provide Nigeria with a face-lift to assuage a national consciousness that has become defensive about the country's image at home and abroad will not suffice alone. The co-authors of this book propose an approach that should be taken seriously by those who hold that a reform movement is necessary in the future development of the nation. They provide us with many of the steps necessary to achieve a breakthrough in the process to control the problem.

Dr. Charles Jarmon, Howard University

PREFACE

A couple of years ago, my daughter, Udobaku, who in her early teenage years had made useful contributions the production of my first two books, reminded me that I had promised to co-author a book with her when she grew up. It is true that I did say so, but I was not sure if I really meant it or was just complementing her for the zeal she had to be part of my effort to produce the books quickly at that time. Nevertheless her reminder set me thinking, because the problem that I was writing about to sensitize Nigerians on its potential dangers to society and to the nation's economy was growing worse by the day. Therefore by the time she reminded me on 5th January 2009, I had already made up my mind to write a third book on the subject. And her reminder came in a rather challenging and dramatic text message, and I quote: "George H. W. Bush is going to jump from a plane via parachute for his 85th birthday!" Surely her Dad can write a book even at 80, to reinforce a battle he joined 30 years ago against a disease that threatens the very existence of Nigeria! That was it! We later talked on the telephone to assign areas of interest which each of us would write about. This book is the result.

Mazi Kanu Oji, Lekki, Lagos; April 2009

ACKNOWLEDGMENTS

I take the chance to add my gratitude to my other children, Nwachukwu, Chinwego and Akajiulonna, who promptly responded in total support of Udobaku's initiative for the production of this book. Nwachukwu, who just returned from National Youth Service in Sokoto state, readily volunteered to type the manuscript on his laptop. He not only did, but also acted as my correcting companion to check the language, diction and accuracy of facts encompassed. A good student of Daddy in grammar and the writing art, he proved to be fabulously supportive of ageing Dad. Chinweugo supplied in abundance all the writing materials ever needed. Then Akajiulonna made sure all typed manuscripts got off by e-mail to Udobaku in the U.S.A. for integration with the second part dealing with health issues. These three children make me reassured, that though their Mom is dead, she is very much alive through them. God bless them all!

Mazi Kanu Oji, Lekki, Lagos
31st March, 2009

INTRODUCTION

Corruption, ethical decay and indiscipline are terms used to describe a social malady that gradually developed when the British Colonial administration withdrew from Nigeria. In the internal self-government period of three regions, 1954 through 1959, the problem was heard in mild rumours very occasionally; but from independence to the First Military Interregnum it had grown so much louder and more frequent, that it formed the main reason the military gave for the coup d 'etat of 15th January, 1966, which brought General Aguyi Ironsi to power as military Head of State. He sought to cure the ills of the nation especially that of divisiveness, by taking the country back to pre-1946 era when the British ran it as a unitary state of 24 provinces. Most Nigerians apparently preferred a federal dispensation, leading to a counter coup d'etat on 29th July, 1966 that brought General Yakubu Gowon to power. He ruled until 29th July, 1975 after fighting the civil war of National Unity, 1967 to 1970, when he was overthrown in a palace bloodless coupe by General Murtala Mohammed as Head of State with Olusegun Obasanjo as Chief of Staff. Reason for this putsch was again to stop escalating corruption and return the nation to civilian rule by 1979.

When General Murtala Mohammed died on 13th February, 1976, after 200 amazing days of political action and shake up of the establishment to expose and punish corruption, General Olusegun Obasanjo took over and faithfully fulfilled the regime's objective by handing over power voluntarily to the freely elected civilian government of Alhaji Shehu Shagari as the first Executive President of Nigeria on 1st October, 1979.

Before the end of his first term in office, rumours were already flying around of Ministers that bought Jet planes or State Governors that bought mansions in Europe, America and the Middle East. The 1983 general elections saw money politics in action. President Shagari had in his first term appointed a National Ethical Re-Orientation Committee to investigate the ethical decay problem and recommend a solution. So on 1st October, 1983 when he began his second term he created a Ministry of National Guidance with a frontline politician of the First Republic as Minister to execute the recommendations in the Committee report. The military were not impressed; so on 31ˢᵗ December, 1983 the Armed Forces took over power in a bloodless coupe, with General Muhammadu Buhari as Head of State and Brigadier Tunde Idiagbon as Chief of Staff. Rampant corruption and gross national indiscipline was their reason. They launched the then popular War Against Indiscipline, WAI, with jingles on queuing and other evidences of good social behaviour and discipline.

On 25ᵗʰ August, 1985, General Ibrahim B. Babangida (IBB) staged another bloodless palace coup d'etat and assumed the title of President for the first time for a military Head of State. He jettisoned War Against Indiscipline (WAI) and launched Mass Mobilization for Self Reliance, Social Justice, and Economic Recovery (MAMSER) and Structural Adjustment Programme (SAP). He started a long transitional programme in which he created two parties to replace the many in existence under which a free and fair election was held which Bashorun M.K.O. Abiola won in June, 1993. The public uproar that followed the annulment of Abiola's election forced IBB to "step aside", and power given to a civilian Head of State, Chief Ernest Shonekan with General Sani Abacha as his Minister of Defence. It was like appointing a tiger to be chief security officer to a lamb. After some 73 days, Chief Shonekan was ordered to quit by General Abacha who then took over as absolute Military Head of State. He quickly launched, War Against Indiscipline and Corruption, "WAI-C", which people later began to read as "WAI minus C", from observing how he wielded corrupt power absolutely. He died suddenly in 1998 and General Abdulsalam Abubakar took over and piloted Nigeria, promulgating the 1999 constitution and holding successful general elections that brought retired General Olusegun Obasanjo back as civilian President on 29ᵗʰ May, 1999.

As regimes came and went, the problem grew in its intensity and pervasiveness until today when the end of the first decade of the 21ˢᵗ century, the nation seems helpless to find the real cure for it. This third book of the series on the subject will endeavour to give a gist of the effort to fight the malady and highlight and emphasize the real CURE of the cancerous malady that now threatens to destroy Nigeria as a viable political and economic entity.

CHAPTER ONE
ETHICAL REVOLUTION ERA
(1981 – 1983)

Corruption in Nigeria has had a long history, dating back to even the colonial era, when the country was put together as one through the amalgamation of the Northern and Southern Protectorates in 1914, to form the Nation State, Nigeria. Colonial ordinances were promulgated to control specific aspects of it: like bribery and corruption; receiving under false pretences; embezzlement and fraudulent conversion of public assets by public officers, et cetera. The young country soon developed a voluminous criminal code to curb and punish such deviant manifestation of criminality. Many of such laws were culled from British local laws into Nigerian ordinances. Even after independence, local laws to combat crimes of dishonesty were framed around similar British laws used to control similar developments.

Examples of corruption at the early stages were those of semi-illiterate police men who collected bribes to let traffic offenders off the hook; or uneducated native and magistrate court officials, such as interpreters, who received bribes in cash and kind to influence cases one way or the other. Clerks and government officers at times took tips from anxious members of the public to help them get quicker attention to their applications for licences or other permits or favours from offices. Nigerian Senior Service Officers, who were appointed to gradually take over from the departing British officers, were not immediately involved in corruption while they worked side by side or under direct supervision of the British. But when full independence arrived and power devolved on Nigerians, temptation to abuse power became more overwhelming. Corruption in high places reared its ugly head, leading to the first military coupe of 15th January, 1966 and all the sad events that followed, including a 30-month war that should have been avoided.

The first civilian, freely elected government that followed the first military interregnum, 1966-1979, was that of President Shehu Shagari, which took office on 1st October, 1979. That administration can confidently be credited with the fact that it was the first one in Nigeria to recognize pervasive, rampant corruption as a dangerous development, which cannot be handled by myriads of laws and ordinances meant to combat normal levels of deviant behaviour in society. That administration observed that the Nigerian situation was grossly abnormal, following years of great upheavals and war of people with varying backgrounds, culture and languages. Corruption, ethical decay and indiscipline had to be recognized as a huge social and economic problem of overwhelming national and even international proportions. It therefore needed to be studied carefully and a viable program of action drawn up to eliminate it before it destroys the country.

The writer prepared Source Documents early in the year, 1981, on the great dangers of not giving it as much attention as is given to other national needs of the country, such as public health, education or transportation. These were sent to key stakeholders in the nation, like State Governors, Bishops, Chief Imams, Natural Rulers, Elder Statesmen, progressive intellectuals and political parties. The responses were unambiguous in endorsing the ideas canvassed[12]. The writer also had audience with key "movers and shakers of society", to borrow from popular Nigerian political parlance. Soon everyone was talking about the problem, although many thought there would never be the political will to stop the menace, because the really destructive type of corruption is perpetrated by the very highest in society who dictate and hold political power. Some simply said the writer was fool hardy, and that it was unrealistic for anyone to expect to stem the tide of corruption which was like an ocean surge driven by a major perennial wind system similar to the Westerlies or the Trade Winds. That was the setting in the summer of 1981, but the writer was not about to surrender to doubting Thomases, who might want to deflate any hopes of getting official national recognition of this national malady as deserving equal budgetary attention as are other essential services in the nation.

Then in November, 1981 at Port Harcourt, Rivers State, President Shehu Shagari announced, at the convention of the ruling National Party of Nigeria, his intention to launch an Ethical Revolution to tackle the dangerously escalating problem of corruption, ethical decay and gross national indiscipline in the country. The ovation was loud and electrifying. It was official: the freely elected leader of the nation agreed that the problem could no longer be left to solve itself over time, but must now be tackled like infectious killer diseases that need wholesale inoculation to control and eradicate. The essential first step has been taken, that is, to recognise it as an intractable social malaise that will not go away on its own. Next, the President appointed an Ethical Re-Orientation Committee, with the terms of reference as follows:

1. to study the nature, extent and causes of the apparent breakdown in our national ethic and discipline in all its ramifications;
2. to determine the impact of such ramifications upon the society and the economy;
3. to recommend measures immediate and long term for reversing the present trend and removing its effect;

4. to examine traditional institutions, customs, values, habits, traditions of the people with a view to identifying and recommending those in tune with the country's social and economic objects; and
5. To examine any other issues connected with (1) above not specifically mentioned and make recommendations.

The Source Documents used in the campaign to sensitize Nigerians on the potential dangers in not recognizing the problem as serious and thus making plans to attack it with effective remedial action, were published in 1982 in a book as "The Nigerian Ethical Revolution, 1981 – 2000 AD (*Selected Source Documents*)," which was widely distributed through the largest newspaper house at the time, ten thousand of them free to top public functionaries nationwide.

President Shehu Shagari's second term began on 1st October, 1983, following a rather controversial general election, nicknamed "Verdict '83," which was widely suspected by opposition to have been rigged by the ruling party. Nevertheless, the nation must move on. They adopted the recommendations of the National Ethical Re-Orientation Committee to create a Ministry of National Guidance and appointed a frontline First Republic politician, who had served in the first term as Ambassador to the United Nations at New York, as Minister of the new Ministry to prosecute the Ethical Revolution program of the Federal Government. Barely three months into the second term, the Shagari Administration was overthrown in the night of 31st December, 1983 by the Armed Forces, led by General Muhammadu Buhari and Brigadier Tunde Idiagbon. The new ministry never really saw any action. The military Junta transferred its functions to the Ministry of Information and National Orientation.

Notes

1. See Appendices C1 - C47 and H, I and J in Mazi Kanu Oji, "Action Phase of Ethical Revolution"

CHAPTER TWO
SECOND MILITARY INTERREGNUM
(1ST JANUARY, 1984 – 29TH MAY, 1999)

A second military adventure into Nigerian politics began on 1st January, 1984, with General Muhammadu Buhari as Military Head of State and Brigadier Tunde Idiagbon as his Chief of Staff Supreme Headquarters. As usual the Junta pointed to cases of looting of public funds, general recklessness of leaders and gross indiscipline in society at large. Many state governors were detained and their assets seized and confiscated. As the din of the shakeup died down, the regime launched its War Against Indiscipline, WAI, on 20th March, 1984 under the direct command of Brigadier Tunde Idiagbon, with its Minister of Information in charge of day to day operations of the war waged in phases. Each phase was launched with parades and fanfare. Jingles were produced to sensitize the populace of what the phase was emphasizing to guide and point to intended response of the public. Altogether five phases of the WAI program were launched during the administration.

Arrested politicians remained in custody perpetually without formal charge to court, bail or trial. Harsh measures, like public execution of armed robbers and death penalty for drug offenders, reminiscent of the Nigerian civil war, were introduced. The general atmosphere soon grew wearisome for society at large. While the orderliness of waiting patiently in queues for "essential commodities" which were in short supply was generally applauded, the harsh living conditions became increasingly irritating. Opposing elements in the army took advantage of the gloomy feeling to regroup for a palace coupe. General Buhari was arrested and made to sign his retirement document in custody.

So in the morning of 25th August, 1985, General Ibrahim Badamasi Babangida, IBB, seized power from Buhari in a bloodless operation, assumed the title of President, the only one in Nigerian history. He rather appointed a Chief of General Staff, as the Chief of Staff Supreme Headquarters title was abolished. He started by releasing all the detained politicians, an act that brought him immediate goodwill among the political elites and their families and friends. He returned the houses and assets of the politicians which General Buhari had confiscated, saying even a Military government must be humane to its own people. These acts and utterances brought a good measure of fresh air and psychological relief to many, who had grown weary of the charged atmosphere of regimented orderliness of queuing, parades and flag drills of Buhari/Idiagbon regime.

IBB seemed to move gradually away from fighting any war against corruption or gross social indiscipline as such. He rather paid more attention to political reforms, political parties and electoral reforms, as a means to inject leadership discipline into the politicians. He abolished the numerous parties in existence and created only two parties, namely National Republican Convention, NRC, and the Social Democratic Party, SDP. He then drew up for them what were meant to be platform guidelines or sample Manifesto for each party; the one veering a little to the right, and the other a little to the left.

Newspaper cartoonists had a field day designing and publishing the two-party political dance, with lyrics to go with them. He went ahead to fund the parties, building secretariats for the two parties nationwide to dissuade politicians in office from having to build into budgets, fake items, which would have to be returned as kickbacks to generate funds to run parties.

He also went exhaustively into electoral reforms. His Chief Electoral Officer, Chief Humphrey Nwosu, head of the Federal Electoral Commission, FEDECO, worked out several voting options and patterns, the most popular of which was the famous A4[1], used in the 1993 General Election, which Bashorun M.K.O. Abiola, won but which was annulled by IBB before the results were announced. The election was hailed by local and foreign observers as the freest and fairest ever held in Nigeria. Although Nwosu has, in his book, now declared Abiola as true (no longer presumed) winner, the reason for the annulment has never been given. Some political analysts have opined that Nigeria's ruling establishment could not tolerate power going elsewhere at the time. Perhaps only IBB can say what the reason was. As of now, he is not saying why he did it.

Nigerian politicians, who are today shouting themselves hoarse about the unacceptable white paper on the Justice Uwais Electoral Reform Report, should rather think of pooling together their myriad of political parties into one opposition party before the 2011 general elections, as in Zimbabwe under the leadership of Mr. Morgan Tsvangirai. Then they may have a chance against the more organized ruling party, PDP, now that the government has accepted the option A4, secret open ballot system of voting that aided a popular M.K.O. Abiola's candidacy in 1993.

For the general populace, IBB came out with a mild organization that emphasized civility and fairness called "Mass Mobilization for Self Reliance, Social Justice and Economic Recovery", MAMSER, not ever dwelling on corruption at all. For the economy he launched his Structural Adjustment Programme, SAP, under which Nigerians were to tighten their belts to enable the governments make the fundamental adjustments in infrastructure and production structure to gradually reduce excessive importation of what can be produced at home. This brought him in head to head collision with American economic interests when he planned to ban the importation of wheat to promote local production. SAP sapped the life out of many Nigerian homes, despite the noble effort of his charismatic wife, Maryam, to promote "Better Life For Rural Women"; which was often read in towns in the Igbo speaking areas as "Bitter Life For Aruru ala Women," (*which translated in English is* "Bitter Life for Wicked Women").

IBB had one other pet program he introduced, that of Transition to Civilian Rule. It included civilian administration in the states, with state governors and state assemblies elected into office. Even senators and federal representatives were elected, while he remained the military president superimposed upon elected civilians. It was as if he was giving them a trial run to demonstrate how they would perform when civilian rule returned. Some foreign observers felt irked by the spectacle of freely elected representatives of the people being made to operate, caged as it were in a military atmosphere under the control of a military dictator as president. One outgoing diplomat, urged him in his farewell remarks to hasten his transition program so the nation could go to general elections for ushering in a truly civilian government in a democratic dispensation. Observing that the Transition Program was lasting too long, he concluded, "Transition is not democracy."

At long last, general elections were held on 12th June, 1993 conducted by Chief Humphrey Nwosu as Chairman of the Federal Electoral Commission, FEDECO, the then equivalent of today's Independent National Electoral Commission, INEC. Heavily assisted by the great simplicity of two parties only, in the contest, and the secret open ballot system of voting, the elections were unanimously declared the freest and fairest ever held in Nigeria, by local and foreign observers who witnessed the balloting nationwide. It is seriously doubtful that any electoral wizard could have achieved the same level of orderliness if he faced the bewildering complexity and cacophony of the life and death scramble of fifty-one (51) parties of political job seekers, called politicians, as they battled to join the elite band of "national cake dispensers". Before the final results were announced by FEDECO, IBB annulled the elections and imprisoned Chief Humphrey Nwosu on 23rd June, 1993. The nation was stunned in disbelief. There were protests and demonstrations against the annulment. Meanwhile Chief Abiola claimed victory supported by the unofficial election result figures collated by independent news houses from polling centres across the country. In the heat of the political impasse, IBB was forced to "step aside" and power was handed over to Chief Ernest Shonekan as Interim Head of State, with General Sani Abacha as Minister of Defense as an interim cooling off measure.

By November, 1993 General Abacha had perfected his plan to assume power; when he ordered the defenseless civilian Interim Head of State to resign and he assumed power as Head of State. Before he unfolded his plans for a long exercise of absolute power, he launched his War Against Indiscipline and

Corruption, WAI-C, with fanfare, similar to Brigadier Idiagbon's program under General Buhari, with brigades and jingles to glamorize the populace. Rumours of looting and high profile corruption in the administration led many to read his WAI-C as "WAI minus Corruption". His political plan was to perpetuate his rule by getting himself elected as President by the five political parties nominating him as their candidate; in which case he would be the only candidate and be elected unopposed! He detained all who expressed vocal opposition to his dictatorial measures and even closed some media houses. Hired assassins were across the nation, terrorizing people into silence. Detained politicians included Chief M.K.O. Abiola, who had in frustration declared himself president; Former Head of State General Olusegun Obasanjo (rtd) and General Shehu Musa Yar'Adua (rtd), who died in prison. Many prominent citizens left the country and went overseas for dear life; die-hard democrats and politicians continued the agitation for change while businessmen lay low under pressure including the writer whose company that depended on government patronage, lost its ongoing contract to another company owned by an ex-soldier, and was denied any further business when his American partners were warned by some secret service personnel never to expect any more contracts soon after his book, "Action Phase of Ethical Revolution," was launched almost contemporaneously with Abacha's WAI-C.

Then on 8th June, 1998 General Abacha died suddenly to the great relief of all. General Abdulsalami Abubakar took over as Head of State to prepare the country immediately for return to civilian rule. He worked very hard indeed to draw up the 1999 Constitution, now operating; held successful general elections; and in less than twelve months, on 29th May, 1999, handed over power to President-elect Olusegun Obasanjo, freely elected on the platform of the People's Democratic Party, PDP. It was a very tight operation and the Abdulsalami Abubakar regime did not have any time to engage in campaign against corruption. However, while he served, revelations of the massive treasury looting perpetrated by Abacha came to light. Many foreign nations lent helping hands in revealing illegal cash deposits by Abacha in foreign banks. Such investigations continued through into the incoming Obasanjo administration, to be discussed in the next chapter.

Notes

1. An electoral system introduced by Nigeria's National Electoral Commission (NEC), comprising of a series of caucuses and voting from local to national level

CHAPTER THREE
INTER-REVOLUTIONS ERA
(29TH MAY, 1999 – 29TH MAY, 2007)

On 29th May, 1999, Chief Olusegun Obasanjo was sworn in as civilian President, with Alhaji Atiku Abubakar as Vice President, freely elected in the general elections conducted by the transitional regime of General Abdulsalami Abubakar, finally ending military rule in Nigeria. In his inauguration speech at Eagle Square, Abuja, he announced emphatically his intention to tackle corruption "head-on at all levels", describing it as "the greatest single bane of our society today", and claiming that "one of the greatest tragedies of military rule in recent times is that corruption was allowed to grow unchallenged and unchecked, even when it was glaring for everybody to see." He did not, however, launch any "Revolution" or operational slogan to identify his program of attack, but set up specific legal framework to marshal his attack on corruption. His administration may be described[1] as the "action phase" of all the campaign by the Federal administration against corruption as a recognized national problem deserving urgent national attention.

The first bill he sent to the National Assembly was, therefore, for an Act to prohibit and punish corruption. That bill was subsequently passed as the Corrupt Practices and Other Related Offences Act 2000, signed into law by President Obasanjo on 13th June, 2000. Under the Act was established the Independent Corrupt Practices and Other Related Offences Commission (ICPC). It was inaugurated on 29th September, 2000 and mandated in Section 6 (a - f):

- To receive and investigate reports of corrupt offences as created by the Act and to prosecute the offender(s).
- To examine, review and enforce the correction of corruption-prone systems and procedures of public bodies with a view to eliminating or minimizing corruption in public life.
- To educate and enlighten the public on and against corruption with a view to enlisting and fostering public support for the fight against it.

The ICPC was also permitted to set up an Anti-corruption and Transparency Unit in each Ministry, Agency and Parastatal to monitor the operations and receive report, oral or written of misfeasance to send to the commission with recommendations thereon for correction or punitive measures.

The Code of Conduct Bureau, which had been in existence since the Second Republic of Alhaji Shehu Shagari, but was in abeyance during the military interregnum when the National Assembly was abolished, was revived by the President. He also made provision for a complementary Code of Conduct Tribunal to adjudicate on matters arising there-from (as had been recommended in the "The Action Phase of Ethical Revolution" (Oji, Kanu A., 1982, pp. 604).

Cases of advance fee fraud and money laundering were mushrooming across the globe and linked to Nigerians as perpetrators. At home in Nigeria, cases of embezzlement and treasury looting by public officers entrusted with public money to serve the nation were rampant. Even contractors for public works received contract advance payments and took off into hiding, either in collusion with the principal officers of the contract awarding agencies of government, or as acts of brazen robbery from hapless agencies where there was no strictly enforced due process governing these matters.

In the words of President Olusegun Obasanjo in his address on the first anniversary of his assumption of office as he cast the memory of the nation back to the long fuel queues at petrol stations nationwide, "The distress, the agony and the shame depicted in those queues was the clearest manifestation of the symptoms of decay in our society and deterioration of our system. And there were many of these symptoms:

• The economy was in shambles;
• Poverty was pervasive in rural and urban areas of the country;
• All the components of the national infrastructure were in several stages of decay and dereliction;
• Our hospitals had become mortuaries;
• Our railway system had been abandoned;
• Our National Shipping Line collapsed, while our seaports could no longer compete favourably with the ports of our neighbours;
• Flights of our national carrier became a rarity, and many of our airports were abandoned;
• There was severe shortage of portable water both in our cities and in the rural areas;
• Our power generation dwindled to absolute minimum and power supply meant more darkness than light;
• Internationally, Nigeria had become a pariah state, shunned by many countries, tolerated by a few and treated with contempt and condescension by all;
• We carried a heavy burden of international debt that seemed quite likely to ensure that most of our earnings would be committed merely to paying

mostly doubtful debts, leaving us little with which to address the legitimate needs of our people;

- Our factories were operating at abysmally low level;
- Schools collapsed, and unpaid teachers were getting used to staying at home;
- Cultism was taking high toll on lives and moral fibre of students of our secondary and tertiary institutions;
- There was fear all round, due to lack of security in all forms;
- There was economic mismanagement on a colossal scale with naira perpetually unstable and diminishing in its purchasing power;
- Our national institutions existed only by name;
- And to cap it all, there was Corruption! Corruption! And corruption everywhere and all the time! Corruption was not only rife, it had eaten so deeply into the marrow of our existence that looters and fraudsters had become our heroes and it seemed we could no longer place any faith in honesty, decency and hard work."[1]

In response to the embarrassing, gloomy picture painted above, the President took concrete steps to redress the state of affairs in key areas as discussed below. He sent a bill to the National Assembly to establish the Economic and Financial Crimes Commission (EFCC) to investigate and prosecute all economic and financial crimes and to enforce existing specific laws against money laundering, and advance fee fraud. By 2002, the Economic and Financial Crimes Commission (Establishment) Act 2002 was in force. The now famous EFCC swung into action.

The President had seconded a Nigerian born Vice President of the World Bank to serve in Nigeria as Minister of Finance, Dr. Ngozi Okonjo-Iweala. She soon quickly cleared the administrative clutter impairing productivity in the place and set to work impressively. She pursued foreign debt relief aggressively, obtained substantial relief from the Paris and London Clubs of creditors, and as a result liquidated the $34 billion debt. She set up a Debt Management Office to keep track of the nation's foreign debt profile in constant focus of decision makers. Later she had to resign to go back to her job in Washington at the World Bank, where she soon became the Managing Director of the world body.

Another fire brand lady of high intellect, Dr. Oby Ezekwesili, was brought in to establish the Due Process Office in the Presidency, which subjected all contracts awarded by government to uniform standard of pre-award review and price verification. It soon became a standard procedure nationwide, thus saving the country billions of naira in fraudulent pricing of projects previously in vogue. Next, she was appointed Minister of Solid Minerals. She soon set that previously sleepy ministry on fire by researching for and categorising all types of solid minerals of exploitable value that abound in commercial quality in Nigeria, listing them for a total of 53. She took them to display before exhibitions of invited potential international investors. Many orders and expressions of interest by big players in the mining industry began to flow in. That ministry has been alive ever after. As if the President used her to troubleshoot where there was dormancy or development lethargy, this lady was moved again to Education, where she had a brief stint as Minister of Education before migrating to Washington D.C. to take up the post of Vice-President for Africa at the World Bank.

The dreaded inflow of fake, substandard and expired drugs from the far east by heartless, greedy importers, which tended to drive out of the country genuine drug manufacturers while killing many citizens, led the President to fish out another legend of a lady, Professor Dora Akunyili, and appointed her Director-General of the National Agency for Food and Drug Administration and Control, NAFDAC in April, 2001. She was incorruptible and uncompromising in the enforcement of the regulations and application of sanctions imposed on deviant suspects under NAFDAC legislation. The effect in drastically reducing such illegal importations and re-establishing genuine local manufacture of quality drugs for local consumption and export has been so dramatic and revolutionary that it has to be given fuller consideration in one of the chapters dealing with health related topics in the book.

For better management of the general economy and promotion of economic growth, the President also went shopping for a top flight economist with courage, imagination and vision to man the Central Bank of Nigeria, CBN as Governor. He found a first class honours graduate of economics who was Professor of Economics in a leading first generation University for the job, Professor Charles Chukwuma Soludo. The Governor's first bold task was to review the banking system, a key player in economic growth and development. He found over 115 rickety commercial banks, some investment banks and numerous poorly funded community banks struggling to exist. Reports from the Central Bank of Nigeria, CBN and the Nigeria Deposit Insurance Corporation, NDIC, showed that, of the 115 banks in operation in 1997, 47 were in varying states of distress. He concluded that the situation was unhealthy and too risky for economic stability of the country. He gave the commercial banks a deadline for them to find compatible partners for mergers and amalgamation into a maximum of 25 consolidated world class, all-purpose banks, recapitalised to a minimum of N25 billion; and refused to shift the deadline. By the end of summer, 2008, none of those 25 all-purpose banks had less than N50 billion. Many have from N100 billion to N200 billion capital, as they continued to issue shares to soak in capital from the capital market. The community banks were restructured and rationalized to operate in their special local environment. He did a similar thing for insurance, so that for more than six months into the world's greatest depression since 1929, the Nigerian economy remains stable and reasonably unaffected by devastating gyrations and panic such as have been witnessed in most parts of the world.

On the socio-political front, President Obasanjo made inconclusive effort to tackle poverty and to redress government reckless adventure into purely commercial and industrial enterprises that ought to be left for the private sector; and to effect constitutional reforms that could restore more balance and stability to the polity. He set up the National Poverty Eradication Programme, NAPEP. This body was supposed to sponsor small and medium scale enterprises and generally to get the teaming population of the unemployed citizens off the streets and working. Either for lack of detailed study and analysis of the causes of poverty in the nation to support its work, or the usual Nigerian factor that tends to turn such new ventures to national cake sharing bonanza, NAPEP has achieved very little in minimizing, not to talk of eradicating poverty in Nigeria.[2]

Comparing the assets of publicly owned and run enterprises in 1979, when he left office as Military Head of State, to the situation of abject bankruptcy of those enterprises twenty years later, when he returned as elected civilian President in 1999, he vowed to privatise all such enterprises, so that the government could concentrate on its proper role of creating the enabling environment for free enterprise to develop and flourish. Therefore, companies like the Nigerian National Shipping Line NNSL and Nigeria Airways, which in 1979 had a fleet of eight ocean liners and forty aeroplanes respectively, but had none in operation in 1999, would not be revived or their equivalents set up for government functionaries to manage; nor would any such ventures in any part of the economy be considered for government to dabble into hereafter. The one or two vessels or aircrafts still in existence were seized at foreign seaports and aircraft hangers to enforce legal liens for service debts. Other enterprises, like hotels and industrial venture companies still in moribund operations would be privatised and sold to private owners.

He also attempted to effect needed political reforms to tackle lingering areas of imbalance and perceived marginalization in the polity to move the nation forward. He started series of high level consultations in all six geo-political zones, and set up a constitutional review body to study the 1999 Constitution and recommend necessary challenge to be made; so that, together with the results of his consultations, he put together a package for presentation to the National Assembly for enactment. Somewhere along the way, some soothsayer, evangelistic visionary or prophet, one dare believes in all honesty, advised him that God was about to give him a third term in the Presidency and he had only to go for it while the ovation for his impressive performance in the first and second terms persisted. This man, who as Military Head of State voluntarily handed power to a civilian President in 1979, had been consistently vocal in condemning African Heads of State who sit tight in power until forcibly removed or killed. He could not possibly desire it of his own accord. However the idea had arisen, he grabbed it with skilful and subtle contrivance to make it part of these popular political reforms rather surreptitiously. Many, who had seen in him the makings of the next "Nelson Mandela" of Africa, were shockingly disillusioned when the National Assembly – the Senate, to be more exact – threw the whole package out, like throwing away the baby and the bath water; and when the President showed no visible remorse for not completing the valuable reform measures painfully put together and incorporated into the rejected package, many began to view his effort – indeed all his effort as merely self-serving; which is unfortunate!

With this sad ending of his reform efforts, he began to be regarded somewhat as a "lame duck" President, to borrow a popular American parlance describing a sitting U.S. President after a new one, especially of the opposing Party, had been elected. Everything he ever did, right or wrong, during his eight years in office was now viewed with suspicion of selfish intention, and therefore fit only to be pulled down. That is politics some would say: Hosanna today, Crucify him tomorrow.

Notes

1. See DAWODU (dawodu.com) publication titled, "The Address to the nation by His Excellency President Olusegun Obasanjo on the occasion of the first anniversary of his democratically elected government, 29th May, 2000"

2. See the Appendix Section at the end of Chapter Seven for the writer's petition and research article on one agency of government, NIPOST, as an agent of pauperisation of the people via misguided public policy of government

CHAPTER FOUR
ANTI-CORRUPTION REVOLUTION ERA
WITH RULE OF LAW
(29TH MAY, 2007 - ?)

The general elections, held on two successive Saturdays, 14th and 21st, in mid-April, 2007, returned the candidate of the People's Democratic Party, PDP, to power in a majority of States, as well as its Presidential Candidate, when Alhaji Umaru Musa Yar'Adua, two term Governor of Katsina State and younger brother of the Late General Shehu Musa Yar'Adua, was declared the winner on the PDP platform. Owing to the much larger number of political parties that contested, now 51 in number, as compared to five in the elections of 2003 that returned President Obasanjo for a second and final term in office, the consequently large volume of electoral materials printed; the resulting greater logistical problems of timely delivery of these materials to the polling stations as close as possible to the commencement of polling across the nation, including stations located in difficult terrain, much controversy trailed the exercise. The complaints ranged from non-receipt or very late arrival of polling materials, to elections not holding at all in some areas. The disruptive antics of some of the mushroom parties, which had no realistic hope of winning but wanted to discredit INEC or create the atmosphere for accusing other parties of election rigging, were also a problem. There were reported acts of violence and snatching of polling boxes and election materials. One would in good conscience wonder if the ruling PDP or INEC was justifiably to blame for these acts of naked hooliganism; but many critics did, and this situation made the immediate post election period tense for some months; and, in some cases, delayed prompt take off of the business of governance.

President Umaru Musa Yar'Adua started cautiously and steadily in paced, surefooted strides to unfold his programme; while the numerous election petitions flooded Election Tribunals and the law courts. These petitions and appeal to higher courts have continued deep into 2009. He continued, generally, the policies of his predecessor regarding the battle against corruption, but brought in an extension by specifically emphasizing strict respect for and adherence to the Rule of Law. He reversed some acts of the previous administration, which ignored some court rulings and won immediate applause for it.

Perhaps this principle of strict adherence to the Rule of Law gave rise to more lenient treatment of some suspected looters of the public treasury. They are no more taken to court hand-cuffed and ferried in Black Maria[2] (*a police patrol wagon used to carry prisoners to and fro jail*), as was the practice under the former Chairman of the EFCC, Alhaji Nuhu Ribadu. Suspects now get bail from the courts more readily, as well as, permission to go for medical check-ups overseas. Critics, who see this as a slackening of the fight against corruption, insist that suspected breachers of public trust need not be treated with kid gloves; but the new Attorney-General reminds them of the well known rule of law, that an accused person is presumed innocent until proved guilty in a court of law; and he should be treated accordingly until the court convicts him.

On 1st August, 2007, President Umaru Musa Yar'Adua announced his Seven-Point Agenda, which he had promised, in his electioneering campaigns, would be the guiding posts of his first term's activities in governance, moving the nation towards better infrastructure, economic development and prosperity that might redirect it away from corruption and fraud as avenues for survival or angry protest to any perceived disenfranchisement.

He listed them as follows:
(I)   Power and Energy
(II) Food Security and Agriculture
(III) Wealth Creation through Diversification
(IV) Transportation
(V) Land Reform
(VI) General Security
(VII)   Education and Manpower Development

(I)   Power and Energy
As a large country with rich, numerous productive resources, Nigeria has not, since independence, shown enough foresight regarding the need to develop adequate power and energy resources, which could sustain economic expansion; rapid industrial development; transportation and other infrastructure and services, which could support unhindered growth of the economy. For example, in the decade ending 1956, the demand for electric power in Nigeria grew at the average rate of some 22% per annum, according to published official records available at independence, yet estimated growth of demand for electric power in the country was projected, early at independence, on the expert advice of some British[2] consultants, at the rate that seemed destined to hit a below zero growth before the turn of the century, as shown in the table reproduced below for illustration.

Table 4.1 - Estimated Rate of Growth of Electrical Demand[1]

Period	Average rate of growth per year
1953-54 to 1958-59	22.5%
1958-59 to 1963-64	20.8%
1963-64 to 1968-69	14.0%
1968-69 to 1973-74	9.8%
1973-74 to 1978-79	8.1%

This curious projection was made in connection with a proposed new aggressive industrialisation policy over a period of twenty years in this richly endowed brand new developing country, whose population for the previous decade had grown at a rate of well over 2% per year. One seriously would wonder what sort of micro- and macro-economic factors were used in this projection by the British experts, and in checking it for acceptance by Nigerian officers, in the light of the seemingly insatiable thirst of the Nigerian economy for electric power, the demand for which has continued to grow at an actual rate approximate to the one of 22.5% for the period 1953-54 to 1958-59, from which the projection was supposed to have been extrapolated.

In the previous administration, huge sums of money were voted for aggressive power development, programmed to build up supply to 10,000 megawatts of electricity by 2007. As this huge expenditure seemed to have evaporated into thin air, without any tangible increase in power supply, the present administration declared a National Emergency in the Power Sector; while the House of Representatives instituted a public enquiry into the integrated Power Project in question. The report of this enquiry is being studied by a 7-man committee for full debate of its recommendations. Meanwhile under the Power Emergency, President Yar'Adua hopes to attain 6,000 megawatts of electricity by the end of 2009 and 10,000 megawatts by 2011.

(II) Food Security and Agriculture

With a large population of over 140 million which has been growing at well over 2% per year, Nigeria has gradually been moving from a net exporter of food and agricultural products in her early years, to a net importer of food at an increasing rate. This forebodes danger, since the importation depends on exhaustible oil and gas resources to fund it. The President, therefore, is targeting the creation of more enabling environment for all who are engaged in the industry. More irrigation facilities will be developed; extension services and credit provided for all who need them; fertilizer provided to aid improved yield; more silos built to store excess production; and large scale farming introduced into the country to boost production capacity for export of food products.

(III) Wealth Creation

In this connection, effort will be made to get Nigerians to choose to work through the diversification of production into new areas. Initiatives in enterprise will be encouraged, so that those who can create employment for others will be supported with the enabling environment to do so. The National Directorate of Employment is expected to feature as one of the government agencies to be actively involved in this programme.

(IV) Transportation Sector

In this sector, the moribund Nigerian Railway Corporation will be rehabilitated to resume haulage of heavy and voluminous cargo from the coast to the hinterland, and vice versa, to relieve the devastated national road network, which is over-worked and under-maintained. All Federal roads are to be rehabilitated immediately, while State Governments will be encouraged to do likewise.

The River Niger system will be dredged up to major inland ports in Niger and Benue States, as well as coastal inland waterways, to further diversify modes of transportation away from motorised road haulage as at present.

(V) Land Reform

Land must be available for easy acquisition for industrial and agricultural purposes for all who need it, if this economy is to grow smoothly. The Land Use Decree (Act) of 1978, which vested all land in the hands of the Governor of a State, will be repealed, to enable those who acquire land to have legal documents of title available as collateral in support of funding for their projects; and for easy transferability in commerce.

(VI) General Security

Sporadic sectarian and religious violence, armed robbery, and the spate of kidnappings in recent times have created an atmosphere of insecurity in the country incompatible with smooth inflow of foreign private investments; repatriation of earnings of citizens in Diaspora; and general tourism development in Nigeria. President Yar'Adua stated that the effort to strengthen and maintain internal security will be relentless. Effort will be made to contain the escalating sabotage of the economy by pipeline and electric tower vandals, as well as pirates and coastal oil thieves (called illegal bunkerers in local parlance).

(VII)   Education

Development in education will involve a two-pronged reform to ensure skills in science and technology; and to support industry with adequate manpower. Therefore educational development will be qualitative and functional.

Special Interest Issues

In addition to these 7 points, there are two Special Interest Issues to be pursued simultaneously with them. They are:

  (a) Niger Delta and
  (b) Marginalization

Constitutional Review should take care of these areas.

The Niger Delta Resource Control agitation has lasted too long. What the country is losing by criminalising our coastline for pirates, hijackers and "illegal bunkerers" (oil thieves) to operate is far more than what the Niger Delta people are demanding in the "Resource Control" agitation. I humbly believe and suggest that the Federal Government should develop the political will to offer the Niger Delta 25% derivation allocation of oil revenues and grant amnesty to ALL genuine militants. The agitation will stop.

Marginalization describes what is perceived as deliberate, policy-driven zoning of groups and/or regions with the intent of disempowerment of a people by others with whom there exist typically antagonistic inter-ethnic relationships and tensions. This can potentially impact social, economic and even military power, as well as access to resources. The creation of states, for example, may be considered a marginalization strategy to give certain groups unequal advantage and access to resource allocation over others. The nation already agreed to the Obasanjo amendments proposals for one more state for the South-East to be in balance with the other five zones in the country. Peace and harmony need sacrifice to grow.

Electoral Reform

Later in the month, on 28th August, 2007, the President inaugurated a 22 man Electoral Reform Committee under the Chairmanship of Retired Supreme Court Chief Justice Muhammadu Uwais, with a 12 months mandate, later extended, at the Committee's request, to December, 2008, to examine the Electoral Laws and practices and recommend suitable reforms, that could eliminate or at least reduce to the barest minimum, electoral frauds, election rigging and other practices, which negate the people's mandate. The Committee submitted its report on 11th December, 2008. A white Paper on the Report has recently been released by the Federal Government and public discussion and debate on it is still going on. This was a rather urgent need for action, in view of the widespread criticism of the April, 2007 elections, in which the administration came to power.

Anti-corruption Revolution, ANCOR
Then on 10th December, 2008, President Yar'Adua came out of Former President Obasanjo's shadow in the war against corruption, when at the Shehu Musa Yar'Adua Centre, Abuja, he formally launched his own programme, the Anti-corruption Revolution, ANCOR, under the Chairmanship of Alhaji Yusuff Maitama Sule (Dan Musamin Kano), who was the first and only Minister of National Guidance under Former President Shehu Shagari, from 1st October to 31st December, 1983. Mr. John Kufour, President of Ghana, gave the Keynote Address, on "The Imperatives of Citizens' Involvement in Anti-corruption Crusade." He said the time was appropriate, when Nigeria was taking determined strides to become one of the world's 20 largest economies by the year 2020.

The EFCC, which is the apparent operational organ, was there in full force. The EFCC Chairman, Mrs. Farida Waziri, stated that ANCOR was envisioned to make all Nigerians to take active and determined stand against corruption in their public or private dealings. The Objective of ANCOR includes:
−   Sensitising and educating all Nigerians on corruption and its negative effects on their daily lives;
−   Mobilising opinion leaders and all Nigerians, both within and outside the country, against corrupt tendencies and practices;
−   Creating a sustaining multi-stakeholder movement for integrity in public and private spheres, through the establishment of a network of volunteers in all communities: Local Government Areas; States; and among those in Diaspora.
−   Important Core Values of ANCOR are meant to make all Nigerians to buy into the anti-corruption war.
−   Some of these values are: Integrity; Inclusiveness; non-partisanship; Accessibility; Accountability; Transparency; Patriotism; Courage; Fairness; Respect for Human Rights; Volunteerism; and Dignity.

ANCOR launched in Lagos
On Tuesday, 17th February, 2009, EFCC relaunched the Anti-corruption Revolution, ANCOR, at the Lagos Airport Hotel under the Chairmanship of Chief Emeka Anyaoku, Former Commonwealth Secretary-General. There Mrs. Waziri rehearsed her Abuja presentation to sensitize this populous metropolis, which was Nigeria's former capital city.

Re-Branding Nigeria
In its effort to rebrand Nigeria's battered image, the Federal Government, on Tuesday, 17th March, 2009, at the International Conference Centre, Abuja, launched the image laundering project and unveiled the logo and slogan for the image clean-up drive, under the Chairmanship of Former Head of State, General Yakubu Gowon (rtd). Vice-President, Dr. Goodluck Jonathan, represented

President Yar'Adua on the occasion. Announcing it as the Re-branding Nigeria Project, chief exponent of the campaign, Professor Dora Akunyili, Minister of Information and Communications, said the launch was a major step towards changing the negative perception of Nigeria and her people, both locally and internationally. She said that the campaign was about re-orienting Nigerians; changing their negative attitudes; making them to believe in themselves; inculcating optimal spirit of patriotism in them; and, at the same time, celebrating their very best before the international community.

Professor Akunyili stressed that the core of this campaign was the return of citizens to the cultural values of Nigerians as a people. She declared: "Countries, that have excelled, held on to their cultural values. Nigeria has rich and robust values, good enough to make the country better; and to project same to the world. Unfortunately, the actions and inactions of a few of us and the skewed reportage by the international media have either tarnished our image or misbranded this country. That is why we want to restore the lost glory by re-branding our image."[3]

The Honourable Minister explained that the campaign was tied to a slogan and logo, because, to every brand, there must be an inspiring logo and slogan to drive it. She very strongly emphasized, however, that the campaign was beyond slogan and logo, but targeted at internalising the nation's values and developing new attitudes in private and public life. After this launching, she assured that government would intensify its interface with different stakeholders and the masses through town hall and local government area meetings, with a view to creating awareness and opening up a deliberative process and feedback mechanism to secure the buy-in of Nigerians in the grassroots.

While advising the mass media to emphasize the positives about Nigeria and responsibly report the negatives, the Minister stated that all relevant agencies of government, including the National Orientation Agency, would be empowered to re-orient Nigerians through aggressive advocacy and campaigns. "Nigeria: Good people, Great country", is the slogan.

The Re-branding Nigeria Project replaces the "Heart of Africa Project" of the last Administration on which $4.5 million (£4 million) was spent with little result, as reported by local media.[3] Professor Akunyili assured the National Assembly that the Re-branding Nigeria Project would be transparent.

Notes

1. Ministry of Trade and Industry Kaduna publication titled, The Industrial Potentialities of Northern Nigeria, 1st October 1963, page 206, table 73
2. Messrs Merz and McLellan; Preece Cardew & Rider; Sir Alexander Gibb & partners; and Balfour Beatty & Co., December, 1959.
3. See Leadership Nigeria (leadershipnigeria.com) publication titled, 'Re-Branding: Yar'Adua unveils slogan, logo today,' 18th March, 2009

CHAPTER FIVE
ANTI-CORRUPTION OR ETHICAL

Revolution is Measured by Results over Time
I) Real CURE is Rigid Enforcement of Effective Sanctions against ALL Culprits.
II) Objective of CURE is a Tripod
III) Special Interest Issues

Ethical Revolution in the Shagari administration sought to tackle the whole gamut of decay in society, but Anti-corruption Revolution chooses to emphasize corruption, which is the greatest bane of the Nigerian society, while touching all other ancillary traits of deviant behaviour of the Nigerian people. One cannot really compare critically the two approaches, in that Ethical Revolution was not allowed to unfold its stratagem in practical terms when the government was overthrown in a Military coup, just three months into that second term. The newly created Ministry of National Guidance never saw action. October, 1983 was for swearing in and appointing ministers; while the festive month of December was drowned in the spirit of Christmas, which in the country tends to bring most activities to a standstill. Any preparations the new Minister of National Guidance made in the month of November, 1983 for aggressive action in the new year, became still born, when the Buhari/Idiagbon Junta struck in the night of 31st December, 1983. So no one can justly judge the success or failure of the Ethical Revolution program. One can even say, that the pioneering effort to study the malaise during the first term and recognize it as such a dangerous national problem as to deserve the creation of a brand new Ministry in the second term to prosecute the attack on it, has enabled succeeding administrations ever after to follow where the Shagari administration was forced to stop.

REVOLUTION
The term, Revolution, as used in this discourse, will follow the definition used in the two works on this subject of ethical decay and gross deviant behaviour of Nigerians in the past forty years of Independence of the country.

> "...Revolution, in a more dynamic definition has generally been used to describe any fundamental change that has been deliberately promoted by man with above average zeal and effectiveness, either by swift, extra-legal or military operations; or by legal, often more prolonged, but rigorously

sustained effort under strong pressure for change massively applied."[1]

The latter category, that is the result of legal, more prolonged effort, is the one that applies here. Revolution refers to the amount of result achieved in the given time. It is not a revolution just because we call it so. Rather it is the startling result in the magnitude of change effected in the condition previously existing, as compared with the given time during which it was achieved, that is described as revolutionary.

A program of action may even have no distinctive name or slogan; but if effectively prosecuted with above average zeal and passion, such a program can earn the name as a result of the great change the programme brings to the situation it is drawn up to tackle. Many such revolutions, after the fact, exist in history. Examples are the Industrial Revolution in Western Europe in the 18th and 19th centuries, and the Green Revolution in South East Asia with regard to the discovery of a multiple year cropping variety of rice that revolutionized food production.[2] We are today still witnessing such revolutions that describe the result of nameless campaigns that produced results assessed as revolutionary, even though they did not set out as such by name or slogan. A familiar example in recent times at home here in Nigeria is the one concerning the flood of expired, fake and sub-standard drugs, which will be considered in Chapter Six as part of the health related issues covered in the book.

Nevertheless, it can be an advantage to give a campaign a name, logo and slogan, where its success demands involvement of a whole community or country in the prosecution of the programme. The very word, revolution, conjures up in the mindset of people, the nature of struggle to be involved, as well as the extent of change in the existing circumstances desired as end result. This helps to galvanize people concerned to effective action.

Real CURE
Any program to fight corruption of the order of treasury looting witnessed in recent times in Nigeria, needs more than name, logo and slogan to succeed. Effective tools within a well crafted legal framework must be in place. Some of these are in place now, like the ICPC and the EFCC. There must however, be the political will to apply the sanctions against ALL who are indicted within this legal framework. Because those who get involved in treasury looting can only be those in society who are high enough to find themselves appointed to jobs involving the dipping of their hands into public treasury, their prosecution rigidly, in full compliance with the law, requires great political courage. Such people, from previous experiences, are often treated as sacred cows, against whom the ferocity of the law desired by all becomes dulled into ineffectiveness, via delays, numerous adjournments and appeals, which are the bane of trial and justice in the regular law courts. That is why in many countries, where such deviant behaviour may threaten the economy, as in Nigeria, draconian sanctions

as well as trial institutions are specially fashioned out to match the severity of the danger posed to society and the economy by the malaise.

Upon the arrest of a suspect, hundreds of counts against him, covering billions of naira looted are announced to the public with fanfare by the anti-corruption agency. Tussle for bail follows. It is denied at first and suspect's international passport is seized by the court. Issues of jurisdiction of court may follow. Court then fixes a date to decide on jurisdiction. When that is decided, the suspect reopens case for bail, when court may fix a date to decide it. The date arrives and court grants bail to suspect. Months are passing and nobody knows what suspect is doing with his time on bail; though he may be required to report at the office of the agency every week or every month, as the case may be. Meanwhile suspect develops some sickness, which his lawyer certifies requires treatment or check-up overseas and beyond the competence of local doctors and hospitals. So suspect needs to have his passport released for the trip. The media report rejection by the court unless better evidence of the need is produced by suspect. After many months lapse, the public grows weary of hearing about the case, or becomes unable to keep a tab of what is going on. Suddenly, the media announce that suspect has now been permitted to travel abroad for medical attention and his passport has been released to him accordingly.

Two years later, either the suspect makes bold to order the agency to drop the case, or news appears in the media that the '297 counts' against the suspect have been reduced to one; for which suspect is required only to pay a fine of an undisclosed amount; or some such ridiculous story. More months and years pass by, and nobody knows if the case is closed and what has happened to the huge amount the agency at first claimed to have been looted! This is certainly not how to prosecute a drive, crusade, campaign or revolution to rid the country of corruption, gross national indiscipline or unethical rampage. In fact it may even count to promote these vices for others who have not yet tried unethical escapades and fraudulent rascality. Nor will it promote the cause of anti-corruption revolution or ethical revolution if, when a suspect is apprehended red handed, and the huge sum stolen is identified, agency officials negotiate with him in secret, as if they are begging him to return the amount, but he is haggling to be permitted to retain a meaningful amount for his own future before he can disclose the location of the money! Others will surely steal, rob or loot, believing they too will be allowed to keep some of the amount for themselves. The money is public money and the recovery process must also be very transparent and promptly reported fully to the public, and not be shrouded in secrecy as a private negotiation between the agency officials and the thieves. Agency officials should have no powers to promise relief from criminal prosecution in any negotiation with a looter.

There is need also to tackle illegalities that may be disguised by a supposedly legalising gimmick. Where, for instance, a state assembly passes a law to grant a retiring governor a lump sum up front pension of two to three hundred million naira after a term of four years; perhaps in return for him to look the other way when the assembly men approve for themselves similar outrageous remuneration; it is easy to perceive an intention to loot the public treasury under cover of state legislation. Anti-graft agencies ought to be able to query such a national cake sharing measure, so that the law courts may determine if it is valid or void as a threat to the economic health of the nation.

Real CURE of corruption and other such vices is rigid enforcement of well laid out sanctions that must apply to ALL who contravene the controlling laws established to curb such vices. There must be absolutely no exceptions or soft-pedalling to let big shots off the hook. May be those so called "big shot" are not so big in good morals, and need to be stopped before they shut down the country! As a matter of fact, the conviction of one or two super big shots is what is needed to scare people away from the criminal gangsterism involved in the massive treasury looting that has become so rampant at all levels of public affairs. If Nigeria cannot muster the political will to do that, it has no business with any anti-corruption campaign, crusade or revolution. It only makes matters worse, when the effort fails.

Three Legged Objective of CURE

In designing an effective cure for a serious social malaise, such as corruption and gross national indiscipline, leading to treasury looting of the order reported weekly at all levels of government in this country, the anti-corruption revolution agency needs an underlying philosophy behind the objective of the cure. Such a philosophical objective must be all encompassing in framing sanctions against those who breach the law against the malaise.

Firstly, it must have the objective of punishment of the offender and therefore a deterrent to others who may want to break the law in future. Secondly, it must have a program to educate the populace on the evils and dangers inherent in the uncontrolled incidence of the malaise, to elicit their support and persuade members to eschew resort to the crime out of ignorance. And thirdly, it must aim at constructive restitution by the offender and for the benefit of the victim of the ethical infraction or offense.

The first leg of the tripod in the CURE objective, therefore, is to punish and correct the offender, in case he acted in ignorance, and to deter others who see the punishment meted out to him in consequence. The crime has contributed immensely in denting the country's image. The collective punishment meted out to the offenders, in a way, tends to assuage the soul of the nation for the pain inflicted upon it by the offender. Hence punishment is always necessary for a criminal offence. Any selective or discriminatory application of sanctions will defeat the objective. Universal application of sanctions is of the essence in this regard.

The second leg of this cure objective tripod is education. This starts from the upbringing of the younger generation, to the re-orientation of the adult population, to accept honesty, integrity, transparency, good morals and fear of God as a way of life, rather than just for the fear of punishment. Suitable educational programs for this leg of the cure objective tripod can be put together to complement the corrective and preventive leg of the tripod.

This leg of the objective tripod is very important for several reasons. For one, it makes for total awareness for all in society of the cultural norms and limits of civilized behaviour and conduct in the community. When this awareness is developed early in the lives of citizens, it is frequently carried along all through life as a character trait, which enjoins disciplined behaviour and obedience to the rule of law. Another reason, equally compelling as the above, for the application of this leg of the tripod, is that it tends to reduce the operational burden of the first leg, in that the greater awareness created in society about the evils and punishment of crimes of dishonesty, tends to reduce in the long run the incidence of the crime. This means less expenditure in terms of manpower and other resources to prosecute and punish offenders, as their numbers diminish from improvement in social behaviour.

Under the qualitative and functional educational development projected in the Education Road Map by the Minister of Education, Dr. Sam Egwu, suitable curricula must be drawn up to include character development envisaged in the Re-branding Nigeria Project announced by the Minister of Information and Communications. Education must no longer be regarded as a means merely to bestow literacy, or provide certificates for graduates to secure jobs. General discipline, patriotism, self-reliance and integrity ought to be fully covered in it; as well as proficiency in technology, and productivity for material progress.

In this regard, the role of leadership can be of great significance in teaching the whole society through the demonstration effect of leadership by example. President Yar'Adua, two term Governor of Katsina State before contesting for the Presidency, gave the nation an example of this object lesson effect in recent years. When he was elected in 1999 and re-elected in 2003, he voluntarily declared his assets in public on each occasion. Again in 2007, when he was elected President, he did the same by also declaring his assets, not just for court vaults as others have done hitherto, but made his declaration available to the media for publication. Consequently, the Vice President, Dr. Goodluck Jonathan, followed suit, even though the Code of Conduct Legislation and the 1999 Constitution do not make it mandatory for him to publish his declaration.

The third leg of our cure objective tripod is both corrective in a sense and positively promotional in impact. It is one of constructive restitution by the offender and for the benefit of the victims of the offender's infraction. It seeks to restore all parties to the positions they were in before the offence, while punishing the offender. Following the legal principle that a criminal must not be permitted to benefit from his crime, the treasury looter should not be allowed to keep any part of his loot. In fact, having mingled the ill gotten loot with his own funds, he deserves to have both confiscated as a punitive measure and deterrent to others who may want to loot too. The loot when recovered should be returned to the looted treasury or private owner, as the case may be. This is the promotional aspect of the impact.

The example was in evidence recently when the EFCC prosecuted a student of Surveying and Geoinformatics for receiving money under false pretences and jailed him. The money, in thousands of U.S. dollars was recovered from him by the EFCC and recently paid to the Indian High Commission in Nigeria for onward transmission to the Indian national who was defrauded, thus restoring the fellow to the status quo ante. Pipeline and power-line vandals who destroy oil pipelines and electric power-lines to steal fuel and cables, when apprehended and convicted should be made to pay for the repairs to put the public utility agencies back to the status quo ante, in pursuit of this constructive restitution leg of the cure objective tripod. The criminal may be forced to sell all his valuable assets in order to meet this requirement to restore succour to the victim of his crime.

These three legs of the cure objective tripod, if rigidly enforced against ALL offenders, without exception or waiver, will surely produce revolutionary impact within time; and it is strongly recommended that the enforcement agencies study, amplify and use them in the anti-corruption revolution campaign.

Like any typical tripod, all three legs must be fully operational and functional for it to stand. If anyone is missing, the tripod cannot stand. The cure objective cannot be fully realised unless all three legs are aggressively pursued.

Special Interest Issues
(A) NIGER DELTA RESOURCE CONTROL
The Niger Delta demand for Resource Control is one of the two Special Interest Issues, which President Yar'Adua listed as two adjunct special interest topics when he launched the 7 Point Agenda programme at the commencement of his administration. The topic is very important to the economic health of Nigeria. Many observers and analysts are in indeed amazed that the Federal Government has allowed this ruinous internal grievance to linger. A possible solution was in the package of reforms that got thrown out by the Senate in rejecting President Obasanjo's third term bid packaged with it. The effect of the delay in reaching a settlement of the issue is seriously criminalising the entire Nigerian coastline, thus opening it up for pirates, oil thieves, called "illegal bunkerers" in Nigerian parlance, hijackers and kidnappers to operate with reckless abandon. What the country loses annually from these criminal activities, as well as from lost export of crude and the destruction of oil production and shipment infrastructure, is far in excess of the 25% derivation allocation[3], which, together with amnesty to ALL genuine militants, can settle the matter immediately. Worse still, allowing the agitation to continue serves merely and unfortunately to prolong the grievances of the civil war which ended 40 years ago.

The President will write his name in gold in the future annals of makers of Nigeria, if he can summon the political will to decide it without further delay.

(B) *MARGINALIZATION*

This matter, which is the second one of the Two Adjunct Points to the Seven-Point Agenda, relates to the imbalance in the number of states contained in each of the six Geopolitical zones of the country. The average is six, with the South-East alone containing five states only. Again the issue was unanimously decided by all parts of the country that the South-East be allowed to create one more state for better national balance, in the reforms package former President Obasanjo sent to the National Assembly. The third term presidency element defeated the whole package. President Yar'Adua may not have any problem supporting a resuscitation of this matter to give the polity a general sense of balance and belonging for all sections of the nation.

Here is an issue, which was first suggested indirectly via newspaper articles in the Daily Champion, in September, 1998, when General Abdulsalami Abubakar was compiling a constitution as a basis to hand over power to civilians in less than twelve months. He never could have given such a revolutionary but practically sensible proposition any consideration in the limited time at his disposal. Events since the global economic downturn have opened the eyes of Nigerians to the need to cut back quickly and substantially on the outrageous level of expenditure on political functionaries, especially in among those perceived to be advantaged in the marginalization strategy, and thus greater economic resource access. One serious development is the startling revelation that Nigeria spends N1.1 trillion per year as remuneration for elected political office holders! If one adds that to treasury looting by this same group one can well imagine that Nigeria is well on the way to certain bankruptcy if there is prolonged slump in oil revenues; which is not impossible with America, Europe and Japan seriously researching for non-oil energy sources now.

Therefore, the suggestion is timely now. Since the country has really assimilated the use of and dependence on the six geopolitical zones for settling high tension political issues, it should devolve into these six zones for "state" governance, while the present 36 states become development units within each zone. There would thus be six Governors, while we find names for those to head the development centres. The head of a development centre would not have the status of governor. The number of Senators can be reduced as well as that of the representatives. Each zone is about the average size and population of most member states of ECOWAS, and becomes more compatible units in the case of the future closer union of ECOWAS.

That Nigeria is running the United States of America (USA) type of constitution does not obligate the country to have 50 states like USA. States in the USA are much larger in size and population. Nigeria is about the size of Texas plus Oklahoma, adjacent two of the 50 American states. Each of the American states has two senators only, as compared to Nigeria's three for each of her tiny 36 states. In remaining comparable with the USA, Nigeria really should not have a Senator for Abuja, against the announcement of Late General Murtala Muhammed when Abuja was created. It should stick to the original proposition, that Abuja is Federal Capital Territory in which all parts of Nigeria have equal share. Washington D.C. in the USA has no Senator. Nor does Ottawa in Canada or Canberra in Australia have any Senator. These are all Federations as Nigeria claims to be.

In reinforcing the suggestion of six zones in Nigeria, it would be appropriate to compare it with practices in some other federations in the Commonwealth. For example, Australia, with a land area of 7, 682, 300 sq. km. has only six states; while Canada, with a land area of 9, 984, 670 sq. km., has 13 provinces/territories, as compared with Nigeria with a land territory of only 923,768 sq. km. Six Zones or Regions or Provinces will suite her better, to save the country from self-destructive expenditure on running the country in an elective democracy. It can be a real "Plus" line item to President Yar'Adua's reform programme. It is practical; it is commonsense; it is timely to make him the greatest political legend of Nigeria. Integrated economic development, like large scale farming will be boosted within zones, heralding healthy competition among zones to push the country closer and faster to Nigeria's economic dreams for the year, 2020.

Notes

1. Mazi Kanu Oji, op. cit., pg 35

2. Mazi Kanu Oji, op. cit., pp 30-36

3. Only 12% is needed to add to present 13% for a total of 25% in contention

CHAPTER SIX
THE DORA AKUNYILI REVOLUTION
Revolution Against Corruption in the Health Sector
(2001-2008)

Leadership against corruption in Nigeria was exemplified by the accomplishments of Professor Dora Akunyili during her tenure as Director General of Nigeria's National Agency for Drug and Food Administration (NAFDAC). She offers an invaluable study of leadership for grappling with a significant health policy issue. In the promotion of ethical governance, the proliferation of counterfeit medications had become a considerable global health problem, especially considering the potential for death from the administration of fake, substandard, adulterated, diluted or misbranded (falsely relabelled) products. Estimates of the annual value of counterfeit medications worldwide in 2004 were $50 billion or 10% of global market sales (Naik 2004). In the United States alone, counterfeit drug investigations by the Food and Drug Administration increased almost ten-fold between 2000 and 2004 (ACSH 2006). The problem is profound in developing nations like Nigeria, leading to medication-resistance for diseases such as malaria, HIV/AIDS, and tuberculosis.

In the year 2000, pharmaceutical distribution in Nigeria was chaotic. Virtually any patent medicine store[1] could stock and sell prescription drugs; and so could small grocery stores in the rural areas. Such drugs were also sold inside commercial buses to passengers as they travelled from place to place within the country. In big cities with heavy traffic hold-up, hawkers also sold legitimate drugs in the streets to passengers in automobiles. In short, medications which required a physician's prescription could be purchased anywhere, including open markets as well as major drug depots, such as famous ones like Idumota in Lagos, Onitsha main market by the River Niger Bridge-head, Aba drug market and Kano drug market.

The medication market included expired drugs that had been exposed to the hot tropical sun for weeks and months as they were hawked around in these wrong sale points. Others were locally manufactured concoctions put together by aggressive traders and or ignorant tricksters anxious to make a quick buck from the very lucrative medicine business; while others were substandard drugs imported by greedy importers who went to the far eastern countries and ordered specially made, reduced potency equivalents of popular brands of medicines widely used already in Nigeria. Prices were usually attractively lower than the genuine medications available at quality chemists and pharmacies, manned by qualified pharmacists. The situation made the non-pharmaceutical outlets listed above serve more like poison outlets for the poverty stricken Nigerians than places to obtain remedy for ailments. Consequently people were dying in numbers after long consumption of ineffective medications.

Estimates of the level of fake drugs in Nigeria at the turn of the 20th century have been typically at 70-80% (ACSH 2006; Kontnik 2003; Primo-Carpenter 2006; Raufu 2002; Thompson 2005); the consequences have been sobering. An example is the case of a teaching hospital in Enugu visited by the International Children's Foundation, where the deaths of four children were suspected to be linked to supplies of fake adrenalin (Frienkel 2005). There were reportedly an increasing number of cases of hypertension, heart failure, stroke; also patients who no longer responded to genuine antibiotics as a result of drug resistance caused by the counterfeits (Raufu 2002). Some of the fake products contained chalk, sugar, milk in capsules, or less than a quarter of the labelled quantity of active ingredient. (Raufu 2002; Naik 2004). NAFDAC, established under the country's Federal Ministry of Health and charged with drug control, had been described as serving merely as a "toll-gate" for counterfeiters to bribe their way and their fake products into the market (Frienkel 2005). Owing to rampant corruption, those whose duty it was to inspect imported or manufactured drugs were said to make their rounds, but "found nothing wrong"; some reportedly returning with their car trunks full of gifts after inspection rounds. The situation was patently unacceptable.

Genuine manufacturers and reputable importers of quality drugs were losing out in the confused scramble. Similar to Gresham's Law[2] in monetary economics, which says that bad money drives out good, but good money cannot drive out bad; the only solution being to withdraw the bad money from circulation: Long established reputable drug importers and manufacturers were gradually withdrawing from the Nigerian market. Pharmaceutical manufacturers feared the negative marketing impact on their brand medications if a fake were to emerge. This in turn intensified the public health dilemma of disease and access to adequate treatment in the nation.

This sketch of the state of pharmaceutical trade was the embarrassing situation on the ground when President Olusegun Obasanjo made his famous first anniversary speech on 29th May, 2000. As he did in other sectors of the economy already reviewed in Chapter Three of this book, he also went shopping for a suitable person to help him tackle the problem. The country had two controlling agencies which could checkmate the dangerous situation, namely, the Standards Organisation of Nigeria, SON; and more appropriately the National Agency for Food and Drug Administration and Control, NAFDAC. He found what many consider an incorruptible and uncompromising legend in the person of Prof. Dora Akunyili, to become the new Director-General of NAFDAC in 2001.

Prof. Akunyili heightened awareness of the seriousness of the problem, referring to counterfeit drugs as "murder", "the highest form of terrorism", and its eradication treated as an "international health emergency" (Frienkel 2005). She employed strategies such as the burning of seized counterfeit drugs publicly, and launching high-school essay competitions with themes on the dangers of substandard medicines (Naik 2004). She embarked on nation-wide inspections with a team of inspectors and pharmacists, confiscated counterfeit products and prosecuted the culprits. From 2001 to 2005 under the leadership of Prof. Akunyili, NAFDAC destruction of counterfeit products was valued at over $75 million (NAFDAC 2009). Meetings were held with ambassadors of countries identified as counterfeit medication sources, such as China, India, Pakistan, Indonesia, and Egypt to enlist cooperation. Plans were also made to visit and inspect foreign pharmaceutical plants that export medications into Nigeria. These initial efforts met with vicious resistance from the counterfeiters. NAFDAC offices were burned down, while Prof. Akunyili received threats against herself and her children. On December 26, 2003 an assassination attempt was made against her, a bullet narrowly missing her head, yet leaving her undeterred.

A commitment to a cause larger than self-interest was demonstrated by Prof. Akunyili with a zeal in work ethic described as unseen since pre-independence (Ene 2003). These standards were also expected of those in her employ. She described her leading a transformation of NAFDAC's corrupt working culture as a "cultural revolution down to the way they dressed, the way they treated clients, explaining to them why corruption would not help us...". Some staff described as corrupt, redundant and incorrigible had to be removed (Williams 2006), while others were brought in, often ladies, believed to be less susceptible to the rampant corrupt practices (Frienkel 2005, Ene 2003). Aspects of her leadership style have been described as very direct and brave in the face of opposition. She also expresses herself as a compassionate stakeholder. It is well known that she had lost a sister, possibly to fake insulin (Frienkel 2005, Maik 2004). In 2003, she was made an honouree of the Integrity Award, which recognizes outstanding contributions of individuals worldwide to the fight against corruption, and she donated a portion of her prize money to the widow of the driver who was killed in the assassination attempt on her. The transformation of NAFDAC under Prof. Akunyili's direction was described in the Nigerian media as a "rewarding study to students of management and leadership" (NAFDAC 2009).

NAFDAC adopted a policy of transparency in its regulatory processes, which facilitated communication and enlisting partnership with stakeholders. Its public enlightenment campaigns continued to heighten awareness and draw support from the Federal government, the media, and the Nigerian public. The level of fake drugs in Nigeria fell to 35% after Prof. Akunyili's first three years leading NAFDAC (Naik 2004). A 100% import inspection policy and vigorous assault on the counterfeit market lead to increased confidence in pharmaceutical industry. In 2002, for example, Nigerian pharmaceutical industries experienced a 35% increase in production. Some companies experienced in excess of 75% sales growth. Others which had pulled out of operation in the country returned, such as Pharmacia, Ciba-Geigy and Sandoz (returned as Novartis). Still some which had been importing their products into the country began local manufacturing within Nigeria (NAFDAC 2009). The tackling of a severe public health issue had become a stimulator of economic infrastructure.

A Ten Lane Road Map for Transformation
The Director-General of NAFDAC had more than just the requisite top academic qualification in the discipline of Pharmacy. Her vision, drive, organisation, operational prowess, and dogged tenacity in following through her plan of action appeared to follow a ten lane *road map* that woke everyone up from seeming slumber in the needed vigilance for the control of counterfeit drug manufacture and trade worldwide:
1.   Registration of all drugs manufactured in Nigeria;
2.   Registration of all drugs imported into Nigeria;
3.   Registration of all manufacturers of drugs in Nigeria;
4.   Registration of all importers of drugs into Nigeria;
5.   Testing of all drugs sold in Nigeria;
6.   Building more state of the art laboratories;
7.   Confiscation and destruction of all illegal drugs;
8.   Continual inspection of all drug factories and import depots in Nigeria;
9.   Continual inspection of markets, trade fairs, and other illegal distribution outlets.
10. Prosecution of all offenders of NAFDAC standards without exception

Registration of Drugs Manufactured in Nigeria
All drugs manufactured in Nigeria have to be tested in NAFDAC's well equipped laboratories to ascertain the medicinal elements contained therein and the efficacy of the product for tackling the ailments as claimed by the manufacturers. Such drugs are then registered by NAFDAC and given NAFDAC registration numbers, which must be quoted on every package of the drugs so registered. Sample packages are frequently collected randomly by NAFDAC to check fraudulent numbering or fraudulent usurpation of registered numbers on packages containing foreign or untested drug items.

Registration of Imported Drugs
All drugs imported into Nigeria are subjected to the same exercise of testing in NAFDAC laboratories before their importation into Nigeria, for the same reason of quality control as applied to drugs which are manufactured in the country. They are also assigned NAFDAC registration numbers that must be printed on

the packages before their importation. On arrival in Nigeria, NAFDAC scientists test random samples of the imported drugs before they are discharged into Nigerian legal distribution network. The result is that drugs now found in the Nigerian market, whether manufactured locally or imported from a foreign country, must bear in print NAFDAC registration numbers. Without the numbers, such drugs are promptly seized and destroyed without exception.

Registration of Drug Manufacturers
All drug manufacturers in Nigeria must obtain a licence for the purpose, available only after exhaustive investigation of the applicant's company and comprehensive inspection by NAFDAC of its proposed site and facilities for the production of the range of drugs listed. This is to ensure, among others, that there is adequate provision for satisfactory discharge of waste and any toxic effluent to be generated to safeguard public health and mitigate any possible environmental hazard or nuisance. Thus only truly competent and reputable investors can now get into the industry as regulated since the Dora Akunyili leadership.

Registration of Drug Importers
Before the assumption of office of the new Director-General of NAFDAC, virtually anyone in the import business could import any class of drugs into the country. Her administration stopped all that, to ensure that those engaged in such importation had the requisite pharmaceutical knowledge and competence to handle safely the materials they were bringing into the country. Such importers now also undergo the process of registration with NAFDAC. As usual, registration follows satisfactory process of inspection by NAFDAC of the importers' proposed operational facilities for warehousing and distribution of the imported drugs. The registration numbers of all the drugs to be imported must be printed on all packages of drugs before such products arrive in Nigeria. On the arrival of such drugs into Nigeria, random sample testing for quality as earlier described must be conducted before the products are let into the market channels of distribution.

Continual Testing of Drugs
Testing of drugs has become a very essential aspect of NAFDAC's modus operandi, not only for purposes of registering drugs, manufacturers and importers of drugs. It is so because other drugs come into the country through smuggling. Such smuggled drugs may not have NAFDAC registration numbers, or they may bear fake numbers which are not from NAFDAC. They may even bear genuine NAFDAC numbers while they contain substance that is not of certified NAFDAC quality. Such routine continual testing on state of the art equipment in NAFDAC laboratories is an indispensable control measure under the new leadership of Dora Akunyili. When samples are collected from illegal

depots, warehouses and factories, it is the results obtained through such laboratory analysis that NAFDAC uses to prosecute offenders.

Additional NAFDAC Laboratories Setup

The laboratory at Oshodi, Lagos state for a long time was about the only fully equipped all purpose one available in the country. Since 2001, other laboratories located in key centres, often out of view have been set up at the sponsorship of NAFDAC and equipped with the latest testing, analysis and evaluation equipment NAFDAC uses for its control operations. Dare devil importers and manufacturers of fake and substandard drugs have often sabotaged some of these laboratories to incapacitate NAFDAC in its operations, and the Director-General, who was in touch frequently with the manufacturers of equipments always made haste to replace any damaged equipment, and sometimes to relocate equipment in a laboratory that is not widely known yet, for NAFDAC's job to go on without major interruptions. It is a running battle indeed fighting to contain the criminal manoeuvres of these unpatriotic merchants of death, who would stop at nothing to undermine a heroic Director-General that is incorruptible and uncompromising.

Destruction of Illegal Drugs

Any consignments of illegal drugs, as fake, expired or substandard, encountered by NAFDAC are confiscated and destroyed publicly irrespective of who owns them. If they are located in a factory or warehouse, such premise are sealed up, awaiting what other punishment will follow after the prosecution of the owners or occupiers. In following the ten lane road map of Dora Akunyili, there is no hiding place for these merchants of death whose nefarious activities sent many innocent Nigerians to their early graves before she became Director-General of NAFDAC.

Continual Inspection of Factories and Warehouses

Inspection of factories and warehouses is not limited to helping the licensing and registration processes described above. Continual inspection goes on, sometimes without prior announcement when some unlawful development is suspected. Such inspection enables the NAFDAC officials to detect such business smuggled in by the operators. Any products suspected to have been brought in by unorthodox manoeuvres are sampled for testing and analysis to detect any breaches of NAFDAC standard and laws. In serious case, such products may be seized, and, in case of really outrageous contravention may lead to suspension or cancellation of operational licence of the establishment concerned.

Continual Inspection of Markets, etc

NAFDAC staff now also raid markets, trade fairs and other illegal distribution outlets, like luxury buses and popular street trading points in big towns. Smuggled items are usually captured there. Fake and substandard drug and cosmetic manufacturers often carry their wares to fool curious new product seekers who may visit the fair and make their killing by fast talking aggressive salesmanship.

NAFDAC inspectorate staff have made big hauls of these fraudsters and their killer concoctions in many local trade fairs in recent years under this program. In 2002, Akunyili led a campaign that resulted in the closure of Aba market for six months, which was followed by that of Kano market, resulting in its closure for three months.

Prosecution of ALL Offenders
One consistent fast lane in the Dora Akunyili roadmap to the decisive control of influx of expired, fake and substandard drugs into Nigeria, or their manufacture in Nigeria, is the inevitable universal application of the prosecution sanctions against all offenders under her leadership. She once led her men to invade the two most notorious depots of these killer drugs, "Idumota" in Lagos, and Onitsha Main Market "Bridge Head Depot" in Anambra State, Akunyili's home state in Nigeria. They routed the illegal "factories/warehouses" hidden in both depots. Some members of the famous Onitsha Main Market Traders Association, OMATA, were alleged to have sent some indirect signals to her to relent, for that was too close to "home", but she ignored them all, snubbing the tribal sentiments which they allegedly wanted to drum-up. The raid on the "Ogbo Ogwu" market at Onitsha was personally led by NAFDAC's Director-General, Professor Dora Akunyili. With her was a team of 350 policemen, 150 soldiers and 150 staff members of NAFDAC (Frienkel 2005).

The seven years of Akunyili's reforms and worldwide applause for those efforts underscore the core strategies of NAFDAC cultural transformation – transparency, rigid sanctions enforcement, enlisting public, government and press support at the grass-root level, also partnership with private sector. These are congruent with global interests in engaging Nigeria and the wider African continent. Health is described as one of the new, near-strategic U.S. interests (Cooke and Morrison 2009). The Bush administration programs such as the President's Emergency Plan for AIDS Relief (PEPFAR) were novel examples of public health as a form of foreign aid, and the Akunyili revolution assisted to raise confidence in overcoming the obstacle of corruption that deters enthusiastic engagement. These gains are especially pertinent, considering Nigeria as Africa's most populous country and in debates that suggest aid potentially cripples African infrastructure development.

Notes

1. A term derived from medical concoctions sold in 17th century Europe. In Nigeria, the term refers to stores owned by holders of patent and proprietary vendor licenses.

Pharmaceutical products are sold in the retail stores by individuals without formal pharmacy training (Brieger 2004; Okeke et al 2006).

CHAPTER SEVEN
ETHICAL CONCERNS IN HEALTH

I)   Resource Allocation and Dissemination
II) Treatment Access
III) Health Education, Attitudes ad Literacy
IV) Aid to Africa Debate

Health issues in a developing country like Nigeria, attracts a considerable amount of assistance from international agencies, because of the serious humanitarian challenges which will face such a country in cases of epidemic outbreak. Many diseases, which have long been wiped out in developed societies, are still a threat in Nigeria. Such diseases are malaria, cholera, small pox, tuberculosis, polio, guinea worm disease and leprosy, to mention a few. Then there are others which are still worldwide problems such as the HIV/AIDS pandemic, with a heavy incidence in Africa, including Nigeria. All these health challenges and the huge humanitarian emergencies they create in a corruption-prone country like Nigeria, where experience in their management is inadequate and local infrastructure for containing nationwide crises is chronically deficient, internal assistance is a sine qua non for survival.

International donor organizations which are engaged in providing assistance in the health sector are various. Some are United Nations Agencies, which are among the United Nations System which works with the Nigerian government to address challenges with the country's development and pursue the achievement of what is referred to as the eight Millennium Development Goals (MDG), a United Nations global initiative targeted for achievement by 2015. A summary of the eight MDG broad program goals is listed in Table 2, a majority of which pertain to health.

Examples of those health related agencies of the United Nations System include the United Nations Joint Programme for HIV/AIDS (UNAIDS), the United Nations Office for Drugs and Crime (UNODC), and the World Health Organization (WHO). Among the key development priorities and outcome goals are reduction of the incidence and impact of HIV/AIDS, Malaria, TB, and other infectious diseases, and health services establishment with the capacity to serve and maintain the healthcare needs of its populace. Another source of aid to the nation is foreign governments of most developed economies which operate bilateral aid services in the health sector in developing countries. The United States for example, through the Bush administration established the innovative PEPFAR (U.S. President's Emergency Plan for AIDS Relief) program, hailed as the largest international public health commitment taken by any nation to tackling a single disease as the HIV/AIDS pandemic. Other aid sources are faith-based or charitable organizations that provide medical ministry as a part of their core mission in serving others and spreading the gospel.

Table 7.1. Health-related Millennium Development Goals, Targeted for 2015

Objective	Target outcomes
Reduce Child Mortality	Reduce the mortality of children under 5yrs old by two-thirds
Improve Maternal Health	Reduce the maternal mortality ratio by three- quarters
Combat HIV/AIDS, Malaria and other Diseases	Halt and begin reversing the spread of HIV/AIDS by 2015
	Universal HIV/AIDS treatment access by 2010
	Halt and begin reversing the spread of malaria and other major diseases by 2015
Develop a Global Partnership for Development	Provide collaboratively with pharmaceutical industry affordable medication access in developing nations.

Source: United Nations MDG Monitor.

Still other foundations are rich business moguls with large portfolios of aid funds which they devote to charity, such as the MacArthur Foundation or Gates Foundation, or international donor support of a Vitamin A fortification project (NAFDAC 2009). Significant contribution is also made by retired famous politicians who distinguish themselves further through charity in pursuing particular areas of need, like the efforts of the Former President William J. Clinton Foundation and the Clinton Global Initiative, or Former President Jimmy Carter, who has distinguished himself in the relentless fight of the Carter Center to eradicate guinea worm infestation in Nigeria as well as in six other African countries. Various donors work with the Government in Nigeria to survey the need and prepare the programs which they fund or execute in collaboration with Nigerian people.

Core ethical issues in Nigeria's health sector include a combination of key challenges within government, health professionals and individuals and impacting resources, access and health literacy:

1. *Resource Allocation and Dissemination* – This is simply a reflection of the ongoing endemic problem with leadership. Corruption may lead to insufficient allocation funds or theft of those that have been allocated. Considerable opportunity has existed for public mismanagement of resources with the government's role in health delivery through university teaching and state general hospitals, and in regulatory management and policies. Corruption is considered to be one of the key root causes of poor outcomes from the National Primary Health Care Development Authority in basic health care delivery to Nigerian citizens. Approximately 700 million Naira was reportedly embezzled, leading to the dismissal of the Authority's Executive-Director, Mrs. Titilayo Adelekan, former Minister of Health, Adenike Grange and his junior minister (Utomwen 2009). Fund allocations at the local government level are reportedly viewed by some officials as money to be shared primarily among political friends and members of the ruling party (Human Rights Watch 2006).

2. *Access to Treatment* – Besides the issues of fake pharmaceuticals and misappropriation of resources already raised, ethics have also played a role in health worker access, such as what is referred to as the 'Brain-drain", with scores of physicians, nurses, pharmacists and others migrating overseas (Clark et al 2009). Many have received government funding to support their professional training, yet feel no commitment to serve the nation's healthcare needs, instead choosing to emigrate abroad, even if they had promised otherwise while in training. This results in reduced opportunity for educational support from the government, diminished return on investment in the education of those emigrating, and furthers the shortage of qualified health professionals. Also, health professionals who compromise their ethics while on good-will trips or medical missions by selling donated pharmaceuticals, providing substandard products, or receiving grant support for clinic

services and health research that they do not provide compound the problem of quality health care access.

3. *Health Education, Attitudes and Literacy* – Migration of health professionals overseas and the use of overseas health services by the social elite are just a few examples of attitudes which contribute to challenges at the individual and national level with self esteem, service, and patriotism. In one survey of Nigerian health professionals, many indicated a variety of discriminatory attitudes towards individuals with HIV/AIDS, such as the treatment of opportunistic infections and even AIDS itself as a waste of resources, or the need to quarantine HIV/AIDS patients (Reis et al, 2005). Health professionals would benefit from increased continuing education efforts such as regulatory and ethical practice guidelines, moving prevention efforts such as immunization from sporadic campaigns to routine primary care, or emergency, adverse event surveillance and rapid response methods. Individual attitudes and behaviors stemming from local prejudices and health system mistrust also present considerable barriers to care delivery, for example, the suspicion among some communities in Muslim Northern Nigeria that anti-polio vaccine was capable of rendering the children who received it impotent upon adulthood. Nigeria is still grappling with polio

4. *AID to Africa Debate* – The question is being increasingly raised whether the traditional methods of foreign aid, including health care aid have promoted the corruption problem due to a) lack of transparency and accountability, b) perpetuating national and even continental dependency on foreign governments, c) enabling indigenous governments' perceived air of entitlement, lack of commitment and clear objective in sustaining the welfare and security of its populace, d) promoting a global air of pity, patronization and denigration that contributes to the nation's spirit of poor sense of worth and patriotism, e) ethically questionable individuals abroad can potentially use AID to Africa as a conduit to hatch their dubious practices, f) providing AID with motives primarily focused on personal benefit (e.g. political influence, public image, business connections, tax incentives, etc to the care provider, but do not build lasting independently sustainable infrastructure within the nation itself). Furthermore, in a climate of global financial challenge and austerity, foreign aid resources are becoming increasingly limited and objectives constantly reviewed in light of pressing domestic constraints and priorities.

CHAPTER EIGHT
ETHICAL LEADERSHIP:
The Transformational Model

It is self-evident to many Nigerians that successful ethical reform that is consistent and lasting within their culture requires transformation. The political will for transformation, however, has been a considerable challenge, and at some times perceived as insurmountable, in the face of constant dynamic change and distillation of ordinances, cultures, peoples, and governments from the colonial era to date. Leadership is needed to bring about broad ethical changes in the nation. Transformation typically involves an application of leaders' personal attributes and skills, leadership-follower interactions and situational factors to produce the change necessary to achieve new goals (Frick-St. Clair, 2005; Friedman 2000; Krishnan 2001), such that followers are motivated to do far more than they originally expected there was a capacity for. A consideration of situational factors, successes and growth opportunities are useful in devising a working model for consistent application in moving the nation towards a real cure of its ethical malady.

To this end, the authors draw upon the concepts of leadership by example, combining various transformational traits with attributes of the servant leader to propose a perspective referred to as the Transformational model. Transformational leadership possesses four distinct features; idealized influence, inspirational motivation, intellectual stimulation and individual consideration (Bass 1999; Conger 1999; Yukl, 1999). It involves the influence and motivation of followers as well as knowledge of self (Jossey-Bass 2000; Kouzes 2003). Followers are inspired to share a vision, and are empowered to achieve it (Bass & Avolio 1994; Conger 1999). Examples of transformational leadership attributes outlined by Friedman (2000) include Vision, Courage, Confidence, Caring or love for humanity, hospitality, generosity, strong sense of justice, humility, and charisma. Distinct features of servant leadership include 1) valuing people, 2) developing people, 3) building community, 4) displaying authenticity, 5) providing leadership, and 6) sharing leadership (Laud, as cited in Smith et al 2005). Strong sense of justice in particular, is a critical attribute needed in fully execution of rigid sanctions and constructive restitution legs of the tripod of CURE objective.

Perhaps we can borrow the intuitive wisdom of a great American of contemporary times, General Colin Powell, former U. S. Secretary of State in the first term Presidency of Mr. George W. Bush. General Powell is also a great Republican Party faithful, who almost got drafted to run for the Presidency of the United States by the party about the time he published his book after his retirement; but his wife talked him out of it, because, as perhaps she thought, America had not then matured up to the point where it could accept the dream of Dr. Martin Luther King Jr., that citizens would be judged, not by the basis of the color of their skin but the content of their character. During the exciting campaigns of the last presidential elections in the United States in the Fall of 2008, Powell, a GOP leader, surprisingly to many, gave his public endorsement to the candidate of the opposing Democratic Party, then Senator Barrack Obama. Perhaps to silence those who might be harbouring racial thoughts, as both politicians are African Americans, he went on to explain that his endorsement was necessary because Senator Obama's candidacy was transformational. This means, we suppose, that Obama's victory would serve to finally transform America from a nation that always judged critical issues on the jaundiced premise of the color of the skin to the one of our hopes based on the content of character.

Senator Obama himself, during the electioneering campaigns presented his mission as that of coming to bring on the "change America needs" - transformational leadership. Since his election to the Presidency, the first for an African American citizen in the two hundred and thirty-five years of American independence, his leadership and vision to aspire to it have been transformational indeed. And six months into his administration his popularity has not diminished a bit, meaning that he is doing well and meeting the expectations of the American electorate. That also means that the change he envisaged and brought on by his victory at the polls is good for the American people; and the old order changed, yielding place to the new of social equality, where the divisive antics of bodies like the American Nazi Party, John Burgs society and Ku Klux Klan become irrelevant and fade away into oblivion. Obama's transformational leadership is reality moving America forward in the right direction.

President Yar'Adua of Nigeria by demonstrating leadership by example in matters of public declaration of his assets now consistently for ten years, beginning from when he was first elected Governor of Katsina State in 1999 as narrated in Chapter 4, is taking this same route of our transformational model. He also introduced the doctrine of respect for the rule of law, while proclaiming himself as a servant leader of the nation; thus giving the lie to the contention that leadership means having the crude personal will to bend or reject the rule to push through unpopular measures. This is not really leadership but dictatorship. We hope that when he has read our analysis here, he will more determinedly veer Nigeria sure footedly to the new direction of leaders viewing their role as that of service, servant leader example and display of trustworthiness, rather than that of lording it over the citizenry and looting public resources at will.

The full emergence of ethical decay in post-independence Nigeria may offer some clues to situational factors that must be addressed for successful leadership. Was there some root of perceived disenfranchisement experienced under colonial rule or "oppression" that contributed to the dilemma? What impact, if any, is there of a legal system based on foreign ordinances, national boundaries subscribed by foreigners rather than a common vision, in hindering national self-awareness? Perhaps the past efforts to achieve self-governance and sustained democratic rule, and current efforts to re-brand Nigeria are already moving the nation towards achieving resolution to these questions. Building a unified community that cares and values people can forge a common sense of purpose that perhaps had been missed.

Since independence, there apparently has been a pervasive pattern of ruling elite, able to continue to "disenfranchise" economically the general public without consequences, and becoming the model to aspire to by any means necessary in order to rise above the widespread austerity and infrastructure challenges. This was especially notable in the Buhari administration, where sanction enforcement was at first welcomed, but later grew to discontent when the level of public welfare or human rights are not sufficient to inspire or motivate change.

Idealized influence and inspirational motivation have been attempted with recognition of the problem and launching programs to address it. However, motivation can only be sustained by role-modeling and transparency that demonstrates leader authenticity and commitment. Identifying talent in order to develop an effective leadership team was a successful approach of the Obasanjo regime. Participatory and directive leadership behaviors were also effectively applied; enlisting buy-in, transparency and accountability at the local and global level was effectively executed at NAFDAC under Dr. Dora Akunyili's leadership.

Rigid enforcement is absolutely necessary, yet it must be balanced with ethical and moral standards and supported by a concern and empathy that is consistently executed. Raising the general quality of life for Nigerians can be potentially empowering and reduce temptation to seek unsavoury means for survival. Education to raise public awareness and shape future generations is a core implementation element of the model. This education must be geared at recalibrating the moral compass of the nation to be able to make decisions based on core values rather than merely a fear of consequences. These efforts can be reinforced by enlisting participation not just within the country, but at an international level, such as the involvement in U.N. global development program (Goodling 2003). Aligning local interests for public welfare with international strategic interests can be synergistic.

Overall, there have been pockets of exemplary servant and transformational leadership attributes, however, more must be done to decisively take action such that these attributes are more widely practiced and clearly aligned and executed with the tripod of cure objective. There is specifically greater need for visibility of constructive restitution activities. The Health sector again offers a good illustration of problems, successful strategies and growth opportunities. The significance of health to overall human rights, as a key part of global strategic interest, as a majority focus in the United Nation MDGs, and as a worldwide acclaimed area of success for ethical reform with the Dora Akunyili revolution, make it primary to explore and apply the transformational model. Herewith are illustrative examples:

Promotion of Ethical Leadership and Governance with Transparency and Incentive
This is consistent with the education leg of the tripod of objective cure. It plays a critical piece in eradicating unethical resource allocation and theft. Creating this transparency and incentive through global visibility, monitoring (e.g. Human Rights Watch, Transparency International) and international recognition and accolades. Dr. Akunyili, for example has received well over 150 awards worldwide for her war on counterfeit drugs and model leadership at the helm of Nigeria's NAFDAC. Besides educating and raising awareness to the issues, the rewarding of the leaders may also convey idealized influence and motivation to more ethical practices, as well as help to instil any lost sense of patriotism in Nigerians, as a part of their cultural transformation. At the local level, NAFDAC's public confiscation and destruction of fake medications demonstrated transparency in rigid sanctions enforcement. The local Nigeria media also offers capacity for promoting visibility, and were very vocal in applauds during the Akunyili revolution era.

Innovative Policy, Strategic Partnerships, Self-aid Initiatives (Nigeria & Abroad)
Local leadership must continue to take initiative to address problems as respected partners within the global village, rather than be enabled as mere powerless and poorly accountable recipients of aid. Dr. Akunyili took decisive steps to coop the whole ECOWAS (Economic Community of West African States) region into a cooperative drive to make ECOWAS free from counterfeit drugs. Policy and programs should be aimed at fostering greater, higher quality treatment access, education and health literacy, promotion of the nation in collaborative partnership. Regional and international policy, strategic partnerships have been helpful in educational and relief programs, however more constructive restitution should diminish culprits from fleeing abroad as a haven.

Cooperative work has also occurred with both U.S. and Nigerian regulatory agencies, officials, professional and community organizations to promote better understanding of policy and collaboration in regulatory compliance. The Co-Author, as Secretary of Health of Nigeria Union U.S.A., moderated In Houston,

Texas an FDA program on FDA importation of Food, Drug and Cosmetic products from Nigeria into the U.S.A. to foster better understanding of regulations, concerns and promote smoother communication and collaboration. This was an important mechanism to educate Nigerian Americans doing business across the continents of potential consequences of non-compliance. It also raised awareness to FDA representatives Nigerian American perceived prejudices in their daily business experiences as compared to what they felt was more lax enforcement on Asian importers (Oji 2003). The Nigeria Union under the leadership of its President Dr. Muyi Arowosafe also recognized the anti-corruption efforts of Dr. Akunyili in an October 2005 reception in Houston, and organizations like this continue to foster communication, education, strategic partnership and ethical reform.

Transformation through Health Professional Mobilization
Challenges such as the battle against proliferation of counterfeit drugs, increasing medical ministry excursions to Africa, the U.S. PEPFAR project in combating HIV/AIDS, efforts of the Clinton Global Initiative to enhance medication affordability and access are examples of arenas where multidisciplinary health care teams were mobilized. These draw attention to the expanding role of pharmacists in global public health as an illustration of means to tackle Nigerian brain-drain. Combat the shortage of qualified health professionals by broadening clinician and outlook to have an international scope of practice. International Development Job newsletters post available positions that place professionals abroad at least a part or even a majority of the year. The American Public Health Association (APHA) recognized the expanding role of pharmacists in public health with population-based health care, community and clinical pharmacotherapy expertise, care access, disease prevention, and drug information (Bush 1979; Vincent 2007), which continue to be applied to achieving MDG goals. International exchange of ideas and overall improvement of health literacy are promoted through manpower mobilization in global health. It should also ideally promote transparency, accountability, and reframe perceptions and attitudes over time towards Nigeria and other African nations of condescension to respectful partnership. Additional resources should be invested in raising community health literacy and indigenous health worker attitudes in chronic disease management.

Entities such as U.S. Public Health Service (USPHS), National Institute of Health (NIH) offer student and faculty opportunities for public service, or internationally through organizations such as the International Pharmaceutical Federation (FIP), representing two million pharmacists and pharmaceutical scientists around the world. Two Nigerian pharmacists were provided training in drug information in the United States as part of a program that provides practice exposure to developing nation pharmacists in more advanced countries. Another initiative was good manufacturing practices (GMP) courses taught by U.S. experts in Nigeria in 2005 and 2006. These efforts are a part of the FIP

Pharmabridge project to foster enriching information exchange between pharmacists across the nations, thereby closing the information gap (FIP 2009).

The Transformational model is the necessary mechanism for ethical reform; its successful execution is found in consistent widespread demonstration of leadership attributes and a complete tripod objective for achieving permanent CURE.

APPENDIX A

Telephone: 0806-847-3535

6, Braimoh Atere Way,
Off Lekki Beach Road,
Lekki, Lagos.
12th February, 2009.

Prof. Dora Akunyili
Hon Minister of Information and Communications
Federal Ministry of Information and Communications
Abuja, F.C.T.

Dear Hon. Minister,
Please accept my heartiest congratulations on your meritorious appointment and all your numerous accomplishments and awards in recognition thereof! We love you for what you do for Nigeria.

As you battle to re-brand Nigeria's image in the eyes of the world, please note that many of our problems stem from poverty. And poverty in Nigeria comes from many sources. Firstly, we may not make enough income for lack of ideas; or secondly because there is not the necessary national infrastructure to enable us implement productive ideas; or thirdly because we are steadily losing or being deprived of services we enjoyed in the colonial times due to deliberate but misguided government policy; et cetera. Briefly, I shall dwell on the third cause of pauperization with particular emphasis on the Nigerian Postal Services as a lethal agent of pauperization of the people.

In the last twenty years, simple research has established that NIPOST, the organ of the Federal Government which is entrusted with the mail delivery services, has deliberately and steadily moved away from such services. Few years ago, NIPOST launched a new postal code system for supposedly faster mail delivery services; but this was apparently a deceptive gimmick to divert public attention from its continued systematic abandonment of delivery of first class mail to addresses in Nigeria, in blatant contravention of the Universal Postal Convention to which Nigeria is a signatory.

Instead, NIPOST now delivers mail only into post office boxes (P.O.B) and private mail bags (P.M.B.), which are mainly meant to serve companies and big organizations generating and eliciting large mail volumes. NIPOST then goes on to license small indigenous courier companies to take over its functions, so to speak. Please see the enclosed report of a research I was driven to undertake to discover why I can no longer receive through the post a quarterly publication of RBC Ministries Inc of Michigan U.S.A.; publishers of "Our Daily Bread" Bible commentaries, which we have used in my home for 5am early morning family devotion for decades.

Now NIPOST has gone to the extent of confiscating EMS (express mail services) packages sent to me by my children in the USA. The latest is a package sent in the Xmas week, which left Chicago, USA on December 29, 2008 for Lagos, with the tracking number: EH 5800 12468 US. Till today GPO Lagos has continued to deny its receipt or arrival in Nigeria, may be to punish me, because I have protested against this development.

Implications for pauperization of this new strange policy are obvious. Firstly the Nigerian who cannot afford to rent the P.O.B. or P.M.B. can never receive letters any more. He can only send and receive first class mail by courier, which is very expensive. Result: poverty. Secondly, money voted for mail delivery services is now used to build P.O.B's and P.M.B's with resultant downsizing from time to time to eliminate postmen or mail runners of the colonial times; when thousands of unemployed youths roam our streets and resort to crime. We are the only member country of the Universal Postal Union, UPU, which is violating the UPU convention with impunity for the purpose of denying our populace a service we have enjoyed from colonial times. It means poorer standard of life from the level of all other member country citizens!

Truly, as you declared on assumption of office, your posting to that Ministry is divine. Please use it, as you have always done in the past, to restore hope to millions of Nigerians by insisting that NIPOST retreat from illegal anti-people policies reported here. We need your help. God bless you as you move dramatically to offer this help!

Your octogenarian compatriot,

Elder Mazi Kanu Oji, MON

APPENDIX B
NIPOST DUMPS UPU CONVENTION ?

The rendering of postal services by government to the people is an ancient practice, dating back to the 15th century. Our own program for such services in Nigeria owes its origin to the British Colonial Administration, a tradition that became formalized in 1840 in Great Britain, where the first adhesive stamps in the world were introduced in 1840, along with the present day envelope.

The spirit was to effect the distribution of mail to everyone everywhere at the cheapest rate, following the tradition of the London Penny Post initiated in 1683. In Nigeria, the British Colonial Administration ensured that letters were delivered by mail runners to addressees in the remotest villages, and even farm settlements, in record time. Money provided by the Government was used by the Post Master General (PMG) to hire these mail runners to deliver all letters to addressees at home, however remote that home was in the country.

Similar developments emerged in other countries worldwide. Interest soon spread to the handling of mail across nations, to ensure that international mail received the same treatment in each receiving country as in that of origin of such mails, that is, prompt delivery to the intended recipient in his address stated on the mail items. The first International Postal Congress was held by 22 countries in Bern, Switzerland in 1840, where the idea of a universal postal union was born. The first universal Postal Convention went into effect in 1875, while the Universal Postal Union UPU, received its present name in1878 at the Second Postal Congress. It became a specialized Agency of the United Nations in 1947 with its permanent Headquarters in Bern, Switzerland.

UPU operates under an international agreement called the Universal Postal Convention, which lists postal rates and uniform procedures for handling first class mail, including letters, post cards and small packets. Separate agreements govern other classes of mail, such as parcel post, newspapers, magazines, insured letters and postal money orders. The raison d'etre of the Universal Postal Convention therefore is the prompt delivery of mail cheaply to addressees in every member country by the postal agency therein. In Great Britain, from where we inherited our own postal agency the Posts & Telegraphs Department, now NIPOST, letters are still delivered to the homes of the addressees between 12 and 48 hours of the posting in or arrival into the U.K. Even in the vast U.S.A., the experience is similar; and so it is in most countries across the globe.

In Nigeria, however, NIPOST is determined to dump the idea of delivering mail to addressees in their designated receiving destination of the mail as addressed by the senders. Instead NIPOST wastes the funds provided for mail delivery services to build huge blocks of post boxes that nobody needs or wants, and then spends lavishly to campaign vigorously in the public media for people to rent the boxes at outrageously exhorbitant rents to receive their letters. Most of these boxes, except the few that companies rent for their business, of course, remain un-rented. Sending and receiving personal letters is itself not a trade or gainful occupation but merely the fundamental right of the citizens the world over to communicate freely with one another and with others in foreign lands. To expect the present day Nigerian citizens, faced by hard biting poverty, to borrow money to rent NIPOST post boxes, and then commute every morning to the post office to check for letters, manifests laughable confused thinking indeed.

What happens to posted letters these days, you may ask? (i) Letters which have P.O. Box numbers as part of the address are sorted and placed into the P.O.boxes specified.

(ii) Registered letters are sorted and placed into a huge pile, waiting for the addressees, who ought to have been notified by a Registration Slip (as in colonial times), to come forward to claim them, if they are lucky to find out that they have such letters possibly from senders' telephone enquiry or so. They must then be able to produce the Registration number (which NIPOST staff now call "Tracking Number"), ostensibly obtainable from the senders of the Registered Letters. If they cannot provide the "Tracking Number", it is just too bad for the addressees

(iii) All other letters and items of first class mail are ignored by NIPOST staff and eventually dumped into a "dead letter room", where they are breached for valuables and destroyed. If you protest, you are sternly advised to acquire yourself a Post Office box! Is it sane or possible for 140 million Nigerians to have post boxes?

This criminal atrocity on the populace is going on daily in our post offices across the land in big cities and small towns and villages. Check the Victoria Island Post Office in Lagos mega city; or the Post Office in Woji town, a suburb in rapidly growing Port Harcourt metropolis, as big city examples. Every small town in Nigeria is also an example of the crime going on un-checked for years now under this strange new policy of NIPOST.

I remember in my days at Hope Waddell, Calabar in the 1940's, that my terminal reports posted one or two weeks before vacation, reached my parents in their "Onyekwere Plantation" farm settlement, in Abia, Ohafia (where they spent most of their time), before I could get home (Arochukwu) and travel to the farm to see them. Neither Abia Village nor the farm had any motorable road to it; but the Colonial mail runner did the job, any way, in the spirit of "your obedient servant" – the slogan of public servants at that time. Today NIPOST staff only sort letters into P.O.boxes at the Post Office – a job done mechanically and not by humans any more in advanced countries. The idle blocks of mail boxes are today being offered to banks and companies as office space, but there are no takers! Check the massive Woji Post Office block in Port Harcourt to confirm this fact.

One just wonders why the Ministry of Information and Communication has allowed the Post Master General of today to pursue this anti-people policy of pauperization, by diverting funds voted for mail delivery services into building unwanted mail box blocks, away from hiring our numerous unemployed youths as mail runners, to distribute first class mail to citizens, as in the colonial past and still today in other UPU member countries. Will the Minister now call him to order by asking the PMG to desist and obey the Rule of Law – the UPU Convention, which, incidentally, has power to override any conflicting local laws? The answer to this question is now very urgent; and this whole administration, including the Presidency, should now look into it. If in obedience to the International Court of Justice we ceded Bakasi to Cameroun, we ought to be equally willing to stop building endless unwanted mail boxes and start hiring mail runners to deliver letters under UPU Convention.

Mazi Kanu Oji, MON

Note:
Mazi Kanu Oji is the author of "The Nigerian Ethical Revolution 1981-2000 A.D." and its sequel, "The Action Phase of Ethical Revolution"

APPENDIX C

 **Products / Services**

Tracking
Result summary
Airway bill: 4161991205
Signed for by: AUDU

Tuesday, February 17, 2009 at 13:34
Lagos-Nigeria – Abuja-Nigeria

Tuesday, February 17, 2009
Time
Location
Delivered – signed for by: AUDU
13:34
Abuja-Nigeria

With delivery courier
12:01
Abuja-Nigeria

Arrived at Delivery Factory Abuja-Nigeria
10:30
Abuja-Nigeria

Monday, February 16, 2009
Departed Facility in Lagos-Nigeria
22:41
Lagos-Nigeria

Processed at Lagos-Nigeria

22:36
Lagos-Nigeria

Arrived at Sort Facility Lagos-Nigeria
17:40
Lagos-Nigeria

Shipment picked up 13:32
Lagos-Nigeria

▶DHL International, Ltd. All Rights Reserved
                              (http://www.dhl.com.ng/publish/ng/en/eshipping/tr
Deutsche Post DHL ack.high.html)

REFERENCES

Aluko, M. 2007. Yar'Adua's seven-point agenda (plus two special issues). *Nigerian Muse* http://www.nigerianmuse.com (accessed March 18, 2009).

Babalola, F. 2008. Economic and financial crimes commission (EFCC) launch the anti-corruption revolution campaign. *Free Press Release* http://www.free-press-release.com (accessed April 12, 2009).

Bass, BM. 1999. Two decades of research and development in transformational leadership. *Eur J Work Org Psych* 8: 9-32.

Bass, BM., and BJ Avolio. 1994. Transformational leadership andorganizational culture. *Int J Pub Admin* 17: 541-552

Brieger, WR., PE Osamor, KK Salami et al. 2004. Interactions between patent medicine vendors and customers in urban and rural Nigeria. *Health Policy Plan* 19:177-82.

Bush, PJ., and KW Johnson. 1979. Where is the public health pharmacist? *Am J Pharm Ed* 43:249-52.

Clark, DA., PF Clark, and JB Stewart. 2006. The globalization of the labor market for health care professionals. *Internat Labour Rev* 145: 37-64.

Conger. JA. 1999. Charismatic and transformational leadership in organizations: An insiders' perspective on these developing streams of research. *Lead Quarterly* 10: 145-170.

Cooke. J., and JS Morrison. 2009. A smarter U.S. approach to Africa. *CSIS Africa* http://74.125.47.132/search?q=cache:5_jgS18PjeoJ:forums.csis.org/africa/%3Fp%3D237 +u... (accessed April 8, 2009)

Economic and Financial Crimes Commission (EFCC) launch the Anti-Corruption Revolution Campaign (ANCOR). (December 12, 2008). www.24-7pressrelease.com (accessed April 12, 2009).

References

EFCC (n.d.). *EFCC Website* www.efccnigeria.org (accessed 2007).

Ene, MO. 2003. Dora Akunyili and the dungeon of danger. http://web.archive.org/web/20060428061930/http://www.kwenu.com/moesmemo/moe20 04/dora_danger.htm (accessed March 23, 2009).

FIP (International Pharmaceutical Federation) 2009. Pharmabride Project. http://74.125.93.104/search?q=cache:I5GX00zxEmYJ:www.fip.nl/www/%3Fpage%3Dp h... (accessed March 30, 2009).

Frick-St. Clair, D., 2005. *LDR 711 One.* http://www/ecampus.phoenix.edu (accessed March 7. 2005)

Friedman, H.H. 2000. Abraham as a transformational leader. *J Leadership Stud*, 2:88-95.

Frienkel O. 2005. One woman's war with fake drugs. *BBC News.* http://newsvote.bbc.co.uk/mpapps/pagetools/print/news.bbc.co.uk/1//hi/programmes/this _w... (accessed March 23, 2009)

Goodling NA. 2003. Nigeria's crisis of corruption- Can the U.N. global programme hope to resolve this dilemma? *36 Vand J Transnat Law*

Human Rights Watch. 2006. "Chop-Fine". *Human Rights Watch Interviews* http://www.hrw.org/en/node/11042/section/6 (accessed July 6, 2009).

ICPC. 2007. A background of the anti-corruption legislation. *ICPC (n.d.).* www.icpc.gov.ng

ICPC (n.d.). ICPC Website: www.icpcnigeria.org (accessed 2007).

Jossey-Bass, JM. 2000. Value systems of transformational leaders. *Leadership Org Dev J* 22:126.

Kanu-Oji, C. 2006. Corruption: Implication for economic growth and development. BSc thesis, University of Nigeria, Enugu

Kontnik L. 2003. Counterfeits: the cost of combat. *Pharm Executive* November 1.

Kouzes JM. 2003. *Business leadership. A Jossey-Bass reader.* San Francisco: Jossey Bass.

Krishnan, V.R. 2001. Value systems of transformational leaders. *Leadership Org Dev J* 22:126.

Leadership Nigeria. 2009. Re-branding: Yar'Adua unveils slogan, logo today. (March 18). http://www.leadershipnigeria.com (accessed March 18, 2009).

NAFDAC. 2009. http://www.nafdacnigeria.org/gains.html (accessed March 23, 2009)

Naik, G. 2004. Nigerian regulator dodges violence to fight fake drugs. *Mogabay* http://www/mongabay.com/external/counterfeit_drugs_Nigeria.htm. (accessed April 21, 2009).

Nigerian National Assembly. 2002. Economic and Financial Crimes Commision (Establishment) Act 2002 *(PDF)*. December 13). www.nassnig.org (accessed 2007).

Obasanjo , O. 2007.We will heal Nigeria. Inaugural Speech by President Olusegun Obasanjo following his swearing in as President of the Federal Republic of Nigeria. (1999, May 29). www.dawodu.com (accessed 2007).

Oji, A.K. 1993. *The Action Phase of Ethical Revolution 1991-2000AD*. Ibadan: The Caxton Press (West Africa) Limited. --- 1982. *The Nigerian Ethical Revolution 1981-2000AD*. Holland: Van Boekhoven Bosch bv Utretch.

Oji, V. 2003. Nigerian Union FDA small business forum and town hall on food, drug and cosmetic importation. June 7, Houston, U.S.A.

Ojo , B. 2001. Federalism, Political instability and the struggle for democracy in Nigeria. In: *Problems and prospects of sustaining democracy in Nigeria*. Hauppauge: Nova.

Okeke, Uzochukwu and Okafor. 2006. An in-depth study of patent medicine sellers'perspectives on malaria in a rural Nigerian community. *Malar J* 5:97.

Primo-Carpenter, J. 2006. Matrix of drug quality reports on USAID-assisted countries. *U.S. Pharmacopeia drug quality and information program* April 4, 2003.

Raufu, A. 2002. Influx of fake drugs to Nigeria worries health experts. *BMJ* 324(23):698.

Reis C, M Heisler, LL Amowitz, RS Moreland, JO Mafeni et al. 2005. Discriminatory attitudes and practices by health workers toward patients with HIV/AIDS in Nigeria. *PLoS Med* 2(8): e246. doi:10.1371/journal.pmed.0020246

Shehu, Abdullahi Y. 2006. *Economic and Financial Crimes in Nigeria: Policy Issues and Options*. Lagos: National Open University of Nigeria.

Smith, BN, RV Montagno and TN Kuzmenk. 2004. Transformational and Servant leadership: content and contextual comparisons. *J Leadship Org Stud* 10:80-91. The Yar'Adua's 7 Point Agenda. (n.d.). *Nigeria World Page*. www.nigeriaworldpages.com (accessed March 18, 2009).

Thompson, CA. 2005. International pharmacy group to pursue better medication access in developing countries: ASHP casts lone 'nay' on doping-in-sport statement. *Am J Health Syst Pharm* 62: 2216-22.

Utomwen, Desmond. 2009. Corruption in the health sector is unacceptable. *The News*. http://thenewsng.com/cover-story/corruption-in-health-sector-is-unacceptable%E2%80%94dr-pate/2009/06 (accessed July 6, 2009).

Vincent, WR, KM Smith, and D Steinke. 2007. Opportunities for pharmacists in public health. *Am J Health-Syst Pharm* 64(19): 2002-7.

Williams, J 2006. Integrity award winners: where are they now? *Transparency Watch.* http://www.transparenc.org/layout/set/print/publications/newsletter/2006/november_2006 (accessed March 23, 2009).

Yankus, W. 2006. Counterfeit drugs: Coming to a pharmacy near you. New York: American Council on Science and Health.

Yukl, G. 1999. An evaluation of conceptual weaknesses in transformational and charismatic leadership theories. *Lead Quarterly* 10 (2).

INDEX

EPILOGUE

On Wednesday, May 5, 2010, Nigeria's President Umaru Musa Yar'Adua died at the age of 58 in Abuja, after having battled months of illness amid speculation that he was incapacitated by his health, and having discreetly returned from hospitalization and treatment abroad in February 2010. Dr. Goodluck Jonathan, his Vice-President had assumed the position of Acting President in February by resolutions of the National Assembly just prior to and prompting Yar'Adua's return to the country.

With the death of late President Yar'Adua, Dr. Jonathan has formally assumed power on May 6, 2010 as Nigeria's 14th Head of State until the country's anticipated April 2011 elections. How this change in power will transition from Yar'Adua's path of transparency and ethical reform to a new course plotted by Dr. Jonathan's regime and beyond remains to be fully seen. Like his predecessor, Dr. Jonathan made his assets public information in 2007 as Vice President. The new president has promised his administration would focus on good governance, especially on power and electoral reform and the fight against corruption. Jonathan stated that Yar'Adua left a "profound legacy" and expressed hope for the electoral process where "....all votes count and are counted in our upcoming presidential election."

Yet there are voices of concern and dissent, questioning moral capacity with the current change in regime to achieve much needed ethical transformation. Moves such as the dismissal of the head of the electoral commission, or the redeployment of the Attorney General and Minister of Justice could be examples of promising steps yet are downplayed in some quarters. Strengthening of anti-corruption agencies and the Nigeria-US Bi-National commission are mentioned as a Federal Government priority. Other measures include job creation, especially for youth, halting arms and small weapons proliferation to reduce crime, as well as improving communication, transportation and maternal health. Yet, some appointees and others closely associated to Dr. Jonathan have been accused of a reputation for bribery and corruption, and as suspects of the nation's Economic and Finance Crimes Commission (EFCC). Other voices on the other hand dismiss these accusations as agents for political destabilization.

For this 4th largest exporter of oil to the United States, Nigeria is a highly visible player on the global stage in its pursuit of meaningful change to forsake corruption and achieve lasting moral transformation, while balancing delicate political stability, ethnic tensions and infrastructure development. The core recipe for success with Nigeria's call to action remains the same: A tripod objective of cure.

ABOUT THE AUTHORS

Mazi Kanu Oji, LL.B., MBA, FCIS, MON
Ruling Elder, Presbyterian Church of Nigeria.
Former Nigerian Consul to the U.S.A. at New York, (Under Presidents John F. Kennedy and Lyndon B. Johnson administrations), 1962 – 1967
Head of Africa Group of the Middle-East/Africa Division of the International Banking Department, Bankers Trust Company, New York, N.Y., 1970 – 1973.
In Private business in Nigeria, 1974 – 2000
Retired, 2000
maziakoji@yahoo.com

Other books by this Author:
1. The Nigerian Ethical Revolution, 1981-2000AD
        (*Selected Source Documents*)
2. The Action Phase of Ethical Revolution, 1991-2000AD

Valerie U. Oji, Pharm.D., BCPP
Assistant Professor, Department of Clinical and Administrative Pharmacy Sciences
College of Pharmacy, Nursing & Allied Health Sciences
Howard University, Washington DC
Former Co-Chair, Health Affairs, Women in NAACP, Houston, Texas.
Former Secretary of Health, Nigerian Union, U.S.A.
voji@howard.edu

www.ingramcontent.com/pod-product-compliance
Lightning Source LLC
Chambersburg PA
CBHW021823270326
41932CB00007B/315